THE MEN'S GROUP

Manual

How to Start and Maintain a Men's Group

THE MEN'S GROUP

Manual

How to Start and Maintain a Men's Group

Authored by Clyde Henry
www.MensGroupManual.com

Aventine Press

Published by Aventine Press
55 E Emerson Street
Chula Vista, CA 91911

ISBN: 1-59330-801-9

Library of Congress Control Number: 2013900106

Printed in the United States of America

This book is dedicated to my wife Janet, who has always encouraged me, and to the men with whom I have shared the men's group experience. In particular I want to recognize, Perry Watson, Tom May, Gary Miller, Joe Keehner, Daniel Benway, Bruce Larson, Kris Howard, Dan Lichty, and Jim Buxton.

I also want to acknowledge Bruce Larson for his support, insights, editing and contributing the foreword to this manual.

Table of Contents

Chapter 10: The First Eight Meetings   69

Chapter 13: Meeting Topics   153

Chapter 14: Men Exiting – Men Joining 167

Chapter 15: Sharing with Other Men's Groups 171

Foreword

For many thousands of years, human societies nurtured groups separated by gender. Women gathered to share their lives and what concerned them; men did likewise. Until, that is, the last hundred or so years in American society. Here, gender-specific groups have all but disappeared. Much of this has been a healthy development. The gender integration of "old boys' clubs" like Rotary, for example, now offers women equal access to the business networking that such clubs provide.

But there has been a downside. Men aren't getting together like they used to. Oh, they may gather down at the tavern to watch a game or converse at the barber shop over the buzz of clippers. But meaningful relationships between men are going the way of the dinosaurs. And this is a huge loss. What Sam Keen wrote about men more than twenty years ago still holds true:

We need same-sex friends because there are types of validation and acceptance that we receive only from our gender-mates. There is much about our experiences as men that can only be shared with, and understood by, other men. There are stories we can tell only to those who have wrestled in the dark with the same demons and been wounded by the same angels. Only men understand the secret fears that go with the territory of masculinity. [1]

Free from the domination of limiting and often oppressive social expectations, men committed to each other in a group can provide the support and challenge unavailable elsewhere.

Developing relationships with other men doesn't just happen; it takes intention and commitment. Clyde Henry has put his decades of experience into *The Men's Group Manual,* an invaluable resource with everything to get a group started and to keep it going. Are you up to the challenge?

R. Bruce Larson
Anthropologist, Theologian, Writer

---

[1]*Fire in the Belly: On Being a Man* (New York: Bantam Books, 1991), p. 174-175.

Chapter 1:
Your Story, My Story, The Story of Men

This manual is as much about understanding yourself as it is about organizing a men's group. You must be equipped with an understanding of why you want to be part of a men's group before you proceed to create one.

You are most likely within five years of forty-two. If not, I hope you're younger, but more likely you are older. Your story may be similar to mine. My story is not unique for a man born in the latter half of the twentieth century. See if some parts sound familiar to you.

During my early years, I assimilated the culture around me. I learned the language, the expectations, and the mannerisms of acceptable behavior. I learned what I should or should not want, and how to protect myself. I learned what a man was supposed to be, and what a man was not supposed to be. I also learned that there were strange people in the world with peculiar and dangerous ideas. They and their notions were to be avoided. I nourished a powerful voice in me, a voice that kept me in conformity to society's norms and away from deviant beliefs. That voice told me to be careful, people were watching. It told me to never do, say, or even wear anything that wasn't conventional. Yet there was always a second smaller disquieting voice that questioned the standards. It wasn't so sure the big voice was right. It wanted to hear the strange ideas, to explore all the parts of thought and question the norm. Because I am learning disabled, a handicap that I hid for most of my adult life, my desire to appear "normal" may have been stronger than it is in most boys. However, I think the desire to accept with certainty our role in the world, and the counter cry to question what is held up as our prescribed role, is common.

When I passed my thirty-fifth birthday, I was successful in all measures of our society. I had a career, a beautiful and intelligent wife, and three fabulous children. We lived in a desirable suburb with other professionals and I participated in any number of civic organizations, ranging from the Indian Princesses with my daughters, to gubernatorial appointments and advisory boards. My days were filled from morning to night and they were happy times. But yet, when I was still, I noticed something was missing. Life then was like enjoying a really good dinner, and then suddenly realizing that with just a touch of paprika the soup would have been even better. I was not unhappy. I was not in any crisis. But I realized that I could be happier.

I began reading the writings of Joseph Campbell, the author of numerous books on understanding mythology. From him I learned that every myth or fairytale is really the same story, because it is the story of every man. All our adventures, while different on the surface, are the same in meaning. The masks and costumes might change, but the components of the story are the same. The elements of the myth are constant because the story is a map for understanding our journey. For instance, in one story "the call to the adventure" might be in the form of a golden feather found on a path, and in another it may be a rabbit racing quickly down a hole yelling, "I'm late." For you, the call to the adventure might be seeing a poster in a book store or reading a website. But every story has a call to the adventure; every story has a warning not to follow the call which the hero always ignores. Every story then progresses through trials to its conclusion when the hero achieves a boon.

As I continued to read Campbell, I discovered other works, like Sam Keen's *Fire in the Belly,* Robert Bly's *Iron John* and the writings of Carl Jung. Jung was important to my evolving understanding of myself and I began my search for cultural paradigms that more closely match human nature. Jung believed that our mythologies and rituals were internally present, not learned. What we now call genetically encoded. He believed that when modern culture dismissed our innate need of rituals, myths, and traditional tribal practices, they would re-emerge in another form. Sometimes they simply emerge as dreams, at other times as various forms of art, and sometimes as bizarre and unhealthy psychoses. But in all their manifestations our bodies are trying to tell our minds what is missing.

When I read about cultures where men were able to gather in the Men's Hut, or where the knights sat at a table of equals, an awakening stirred inside me. I became convinced that our current culture lacked key elements. I knew something was missing in my life, and that something was my own circle of men, companions with whom I would feel a kinship deeper than the numerous acquaintances I currently had. My new friendships would not be dependent on what I did, where I worked, or how I lived. I wasn't even sure what such relationships would be or feel like, but I knew that they had to exist. If Carl Jung and Joseph Campbell were right, I was not the only man who knew it.

While I had great social relationships, I also knew that every acquaintance had an additional agenda that prevented me from simply being myself. At work, I was either managing people or impressing them. To the people I managed, I was the judge of their performance and responsible to reward them according to their contributions to the firm that employed me. Being open or vulnerable would weaken my ability as a manager. If I did not manage the people I knew at work, then I needed to impress them. I needed to prove to my superiors both my present worth and potential value. Showing weakness, fear, or strong emotions could have negative consequences.

What about my peers? We ate together, drank together, and partied, but at our cores we competed with each other for advancement. The two other categories of relationships were clients, who I served, and suppliers of goods or services, who served the firm. I do not mean in any way to cast this strange dance of corporate structure in a negative light. It is a useful operational structure but it is not an authentic community; it is a business organization. And while it does not need to be false or insensitive, and while it can be a very positive experience, it also cannot be an open place where everyone is free to display their emotions. If you're passed over for a promotion, you smile and sincerely congratulate the winner and praise the wisdom of the promoters. But if you were free, you might scream, rant, and rave first. I knew at work to keep a stiff upper lip. Relationships at the work place should not be mistaken, as they so often are, for friendships. At work we are not really free to be our authentic self.

I thought back to college. There, with other students, we had no agendas. We were not competing for advancement, trying to win repeat business, or make a new sale. Then we were able to be ourselves without consequence. Other men have told me this was true for them during their military experience when they were with men of the same rank and were not planning a military career.

A month after I turned forty, I decided that I wanted to be part of a community, a group of men that would be safe, supportive, and honest. This is where my adventure began. I tacked a letter-sized poster to the bulletin board at a local library and three bookstores, announcing that I wanted to form a men's group. This was, for me, not without risk. The senior partners where I was a junior partner would not have looked kindly on this endeavor. For them it would have conjured up images of therapeutic rehab and inadequacy, or strange cult drumming, sweat lodges, and dancing shirtless around a blazing bonfire. It would most likely have cost me any further advancement, and perhaps even my job. I was scared. I was also frightened of what other men might think reading my poster, and of what my yearning to be part of such a group meant.

The first man contacted me. He was a professional, almost my same age. We talked and found that while on the surface our journeys were different, our internal journeys were identical. Campbell was right; we were two men, the same under our social masks. He agreed to pin up more posters.

Then a third man contacted us, then more, until we had nine men. We had no idea what we were doing. We were all scared, a bit inhibited, and because our society told us that this was something odd, we felt awkward. I was very thankful that my wife was very supportive. I don't think I could have proceeded without her encouragement. But each of us knew that we had resisted the internal voice of convention, and instead had listened to the wee tiny voice that told each of us to take a chance and begin this adventure.

Chapter 2:
What is a Men's Group?

A men's group is a special form of community. It is a community that meets a man's desire and need for intimate kinship, support, and loyalty. Tal Ben-Shahar, Ph.D., writes in *Happier*, "Having people about whom we care and who care about us to share our lives with – to share the events and thoughts and feeling in our lives – intensifies our experience of meaning, consoles us in our pain, deepens our sense of delight in the world." This is what a men's group is. It is men with whom we share our lives, with no other hope of gain or fear of loss. In our group we say: "We are a brotherhood witnessing to each other's lives with acceptance, support, and authenticity."

The research of Ed Diener and Martin Seligman proved that the only external difference between "very happy people" and what they call "less happy people" was that the men who were living an enjoyable life had "rich and satisfying social relationships." It wasn't money, health, power, or appearance. It was the kind of social relationships they had. How do such social relationships form, and why do these connections make us happy?

Let me offer a simple theory. During humanity's long existence we developed the emotional framework that we needed for survival. Our emotional framework includes loving our partner, reproducing, nurturing children, sharing the product of the hunt or found food, and a whole array of other behaviors. One of these emotionally-motivated behaviors is to be bonded with other men in small tribal units.

We no longer live in small clans where a dozen men gathered in the Men's Hut. We live in a mega-scale society; our cultural units consist of millions or hundreds of millions rather than a few dozen people. These changes have occurred over the last 12,000 years - a very short time relative to our time on the planet. This short time span is not enough for us to have changed our emotional composition. Just as we still need nutrients that are similar to those our ancestors consumed, we also need social units that meet our genetic emotional needs. Attempts to deny the body nutrients will always result in unhealthy bodies. Our bodies may survive, but they will not be bodies filled with vitality. Likewise, denying a man the community structures required by his emotional framework will leave him desperately searching to fill this missing element. A man can have the love of a wonderful partner, a beautiful family, a steady income, security, and even power, but there will still be something more that he needs in order to enjoy the complete life. Aristotle, the ancient Greek philosopher, wrote: "Without friendship, no happiness is possible."

If it is authentic, the contemporary men's group fulfills this natural need. It is the modern equivalent of the tribal "Men's Hut." It is the place of kinship, where a man is not his occupation, his income, his athletic prowess, or his achievements. It is a place where he can remove his armor, lift the mask from his face, and simply be a man.

While there are many kinds of men's groups, there are certain attributes that must be present for a group to fulfill men's emotional need. These qualities can be found in men's groups in remote regions of Brazil, on the ancient plains of Siberia, or at a gathering of men in a local library's community room in the American Midwest. A men's group is a small gathering of men, between 6 to 12 men that meet frequently. The meeting begins with a signal that this time is exceptional. During the meeting the authentic self is present and shared. It ends with a custom that signals the closing. The leadership of the group is shared. Everyone has equal ownership of his group and must be responsible for its wellbeing.

An Authentic Men's Group

What is the difference between an authentic men's group and a men's organization?

Carl Jung talks of archetypal elements in cultures. By this he means rituals, myths, institutions, and even architectural forms that exist in every culture. An authentic men's group is an archetypal element of every healthy society. By an authentic men's group I mean a men's group that meets the genetically encoded needs of men for tribal bonding. Like a healthy diet, such a group must include all the elements that we need for vitality with as few toxins as possible.

Just as many modern foods have been invented for our bodies, not all have been successful in producing healthy individuals. Many have been promoted because their use benefited someone financially or politically. Sometimes well-meaning people have proposed odd diets that became popular but failed in their basic nutrition. Likewise, men's groups have taken on a thousand different forms in attempts to meet our basic need.

Leo Tolstoy wrote in *Anna Karenina*, "Happy families are all alike; every unhappy family is unhappy in its own way." Likewise, authentic men's groups from ancient times to present are successful in the same ways, whereas failed men's organizations founder in many ways.

At the turn of the twentieth century in America, it is estimated that over 90% of white adult men belonged to what is commonly called a secret men's society. I believe that men of other races also belonged to similar groups, but membership is more difficult to track. One of the most common secret societies was the Masons. Similar men's organizations, perhaps less secret but still comparable in structure, were the Elks, the Moose, I.O.O.F, Knights of Columbus, and many others. On campuses secret male organizations abounded and included the Skull and Bones Club, the Owl Society, and the Order of the Crown. Men formed such groups to search for "Truth and Wisdom" (both with capital letters). It was a time when Archeology was growing in prominence, and the rediscovery of ancient texts that began in the Renaissance was still reinvigorating philosophy. These men believed "Truth and Wisdom" could be found in ancient writings or clairvoyant revelations. Also popular during the latter half of the century were men's service organizations such as the Lion's Club, Kiwanis Club, and Rotary International. These had a mission "to better the condition of mankind." Unfortunately, these male societies were the victims of their own success. As they rose in importance, size, and influence, men were drawn to the groups for career advancement, business connections, or social and political advantage, until the original goals were lost. New groups, if successful, went through a similar life cycle.

By the 1960's, these organizations were large dinosaurs that had become intractable. Further, they were created during a time when racism was considered to be scientific and a benefit to society. Therefore, they had built racism into their charters. These groups, whose members once claimed to be searching for enlightenment, became dark institutions unable to free themselves from their own doctrine. They were unwilling to adapt to changes in the society around them. As the world evolved, men no longer wanted to be part of a group which espoused and engaged in racism and intolerance. The social and economic advantages lessened and then reversed. At one time, a politician who did not belong to one of these groups would have had a difficult time being elected. By the 1980's, if it was discovered that he was a member, he would most likely face defeat.

Simultaneously, the women's movement rightfully demanded entry into groups, such as the Rotary Club, that were primarily established as a mechanism for business networking. Many of the men's clubs, health clubs, golf clubs, male faculty clubs, and male professional organizations also fully and rightfully integrated, both in regard to race and gender. I applaud these changes. I also want to recognize that most clubs have changed policies regarding race. I do not want to discourage anyone from joining service organizations. They are of great benefit to the society and the individual. But they will not meet your basic need for an authentic tribal-like men's group.

These organizations, no matter how beneficial they are, were not communities designed to create a sacred place where men were free to be themselves without consequence and without other agendas. Many had become or were always designed to be political organizations intended to disadvantage non-members and give advantages to members.

In their wake, smaller groups began to form. Some of these smaller groups attempted to mimic groups that were emerging in the women's movement. Women might have a better ability to spontaneously form groups. It appears to me that there has always been an abundance of small and intimate women's groups. Because traditionally there was little political advantage to belonging to them, they had not fallen into the same developmental cycles as did large male institutions. In addition, during the early era of the women's movement, many new women's groups formed to provide support and a safe community of friends. But I am writing a men's group manual, so I will speak of men, knowing that the same may hold true for both genders.

During the 1970's, some men came to understand that we have an incurable longing for a tribe and set about to find a structure that worked. Some of these experiments in forming a new kind of men's group were innovative and daring. Many were not successful, but a few were. Some of the groups that emerged from this first generation of men's groups were largely reactions to the women's movement, and were started by men who had been involved in that movement. Some wanted what they saw women had found in these groups. Others were therapeutic groups for recovery from specific difficulties like drug addiction or combat-related syndromes; some were general support groups. Early groups were sometimes initiated as a therapeutic group that then evolved. About this time Bill Kauth, the co-founder of the ManKind Project, published *A Circle of Men*; this was the first book that I know of to include information on starting a group. These groups were fertile grounds for discovering how men's groups functioned - what worked and what didn't. Seven factors proved to be important to the success of a men's group.

Seven Factors for Success

1. *Men Only*: Because the groups are exclusively male, the men behave differently than they do when women are present. Even the most self-actualized and grounded man acts differently in a mixed group. I have attended sweat lodge ceremonies that are mixed and those that are all male. Each group had a different aura present. The fact that humans, both male and female humans, have consistently sought out and formed single-sex groups attests to the desire for and importance of such groups.

2. *Small Size*: The best size is around ten men. The group is an intimate relationship that is exclusive to small groups of men, and that nurtures the soul in an irreplaceable way. The size of a men's group should be at least 5 and not larger than 12. Human tribes for 300,000 years consisted of about 18 to 36 people. Assuming that about half the tribe was female, the tribe would then include 9 to 18 males. After subtracting the number of boys too young to be initiated into the men's group, the number of men was somewhere between 5 and 12 adults. For any number of reasons, including the efficient production of food, security, and professional specialization, larger human organizations and communities have developed over the past 12,000 years, a small fraction of human existence. Our

genetic, internal need for a tribe and for a men's group remains as vital to us as it was for our ancestors on the Serengeti Plains.

3. *Ownership*: No one can be permanently in charge. While a leader is needed to moderate each meeting, leadership must rotate and responsibility must be shared. Each man who joins the group is responsible for its success and must be equally invested. Therefore, each man must hold the gathering's leader responsible. It cannot be the group that someone started. It must be the group that each man shared starting and that each man owns.

In business, members of a partnership often each sign on security notes. If the business fails each man is 100% responsible for the debt. He is not just fractionally responsible for his share. Therefore, he is careful in joining the partnership, holds the others responsible to complete their tasks, and is committed to the success of the enterprise. If it fails, no matter what happened, a partner cannot claim it was anyone else's fault. He is responsible for the total obligation. Likewise, a man's investment in a men's group requires him to be 100% responsible for the outcome. If the group fails, it is usually because each man failed to hold the others responsible.

4. *Frequent Meetings*: It is not an accident that many religious groups meet at least once a week. As with size, I think that certain time intervals are also critical to success and grounded in our basic human attributes. Our nervous system grows and forms new connections with frequent contact. Just as repetition triggers our neural pathways to potentiate, forming new connections, frequent meetings contribute to durable intense bonds that are impossible to achieve in any other way. Someday, neurologists may demonstrate that friendships and building trust requires frequent, repetitious contact. I believe this is particularly true as relationships are first forming.

5. *Commonality*: The people of every tribe share similarities; so do the men of a successful men's group. The tribe members might all have the same tattoo, be descended from the same hero, or worship the same god. It does not matter what is shared so much as it matters that there is some strong sense of commonality. Something must be similar in the other man, so that we recognize that shared something in ourselves. It may be shared values; or it may simply be interests such as having read the same books or enjoyed the same movies.

One sociologist studied the extras hired for the big Civil War battle scene in a movie. He noticed that during breaks all the men grouped together according to the uniform they had been given. The officers of the Union Army gathered together, and the Confederate officers gathered together on the other side of the set. The cavalrymen and the artillerymen gathered in their separate groups. These men were from every walk of life and may have shared nothing else in common, but they formed groups with other men according to their most obvious similarity. Men need some point of contact, no matter how odd or irrelevant it might be. This is not to suggest that any trivial similarity will suffice; you must be able to see some aspects of yourself in the other men in order to explore further your commonalities and differences.

6. *Group of Equals:* Each man must be equally willing to do the work of the group. Each man must be willing to be the leader of the group and take ownership. Each man must be willing to protect the group, and defend his place in it.

7. *Being the Authentic Self:* This commitment is of utmost importance. Each man must be responsible to be his genuine self, and when he reveals his authentic self it must be without consequences for him. Civilization is designed to prevent men from being authentic. Cultures design manners and prescribe mannerisms so that we can effectively waltz our way through our daily activities. Protecting oneself and being guarded in the occasionally hostile outside world is necessary. However, every man should have a safe place where he can remove his armor, unafraid to espouse the real self with all its vulnerabilities and virtues.

Out of this understanding, the restoration of men's groups has emerged. Men drawn to a men's group today are not broken and in need of fixing. We are men with the confidence and sensitivity to recognize what we want and to boldly commit to forming a bond with other men in what is often called an intentional community. When a group is successful, men supported by each other may want to examine and understand their damaged parts, to celebrate their healing, their strengths, or their journey. They do so understanding that their companions are not their healers, their priests, or their saviors. They are co-adventurers with whom they can share their voyage. Normally, such sharing results in better understanding of each other and of our own journey, but sometimes it just enhances time together. Either result is a success.

A successful men's <u>group</u> can be distinguished from a successful men's <u>organization</u> in many ways. Most organizations want to grow, thinking that if they do so they will achieve some kind of a goal. A successful men's group, once formed, is closed. Men who enjoy these benefits do not have a driving desire to bring new men into their group. Many of the groups have been stable for decades, losing a member occasionally only due to death or relocation. Many of these groups function quietly, in some cases they don't even call themselves a group or recognize themselves as one. The small size of the group protects it from becoming a networking opportunity or having any social or political power. Externally powerless, it can be one of the most influential forces in a man's personal life. This book is designed to show how to form a men's group that will meet the seven essential attributes of an intentional community of men.

A Typical Men's Group Meeting

The meeting's opening ritual is a brief reporting round during which each man will "check-in" by telling the group what he is feeling at the moment and what has occurred in his life over the past week. Each man's check-in should last no more than five minutes. Then the gathering will move in different directions depending on what has been said during check-in. If anyone needs more time devoted to a personal issue that is confronting him, he asks for the time. The man tells the others what kind of feedback he wants: advice, support, or just to be heard. The needs of a brother are always a priority. If no individual asks for time to deal with a specific issue, then the gathering continues according to the agenda developed by that meeting's leader. The group might discuss specific emotional, spiritual, political, or other topics, share poetry, view a thought-provoking documentary, participate in a drumming session, take a hike, or other activities. In short, the meeting can include any discussion or activity that the leader thinks is worthwhile. It is time spent together, time sharing thoughts, feelings, and experiences. The gathering then closes with another ritual. Here the manual suggests a short round where every man again speaks. He might thank the leader for the meeting; he might share how the activity or discussion affected him, or what he learned from discussing another man's needs or feelings. The final accent on the close might be a group hug, hand tap or a group cheer, something to symbolize that the circle is closed and that each man will be returning to the world outside his symbolic Men's Hut.

The gatherings themselves may seem simple, but so is healthy food. Fresh naturally-grown produce is good for the body and simple togetherness - free from the burdens, pretense and pressures of current society - is invigorating. Over the many decades that these groups stay bonded, the relationships formed are the strongest that many men will know. The men feel at liberty to call on one another throughout the week. In addition, the men know that these friendships are not dependent on other social conditions. For example, if a man is fired from his job, he can expect to lose most of the relationships he has had with his co-workers. They will have to choose between loyalty to their work or to him. But the men of his group will be constant.

The security of a brotherhood without consequence for being oneself is a key element for personal happiness. It also can improve many other aspects of a man's life outside of the group, from better family relationships to increased work satisfaction.

Establishing a Men's Group

Many of the current top-selling books on happiness recognize that intimate same-sex friends are key elements of the happy life; however, they don't tell you how to create them. This manual provides a clear pathway to this goal. It is based on over twenty years of involvement with men's groups, research, and conversations with men who have been involved with successful and unsuccessful groups. Like a men's group itself, the procedures are simple and straightforward. Following are the five main steps of the process. There will be details on each step in later chapters.

Five Steps to Forming Your Group

1. For a group to bond and stay together there must be some commonalties. Decide what topics, activities, or issues you are interested in, and how to succinctly describe them in a few words. Write them down.

2. Issue an invitation for men with similar interests to join you. You can post invitations on bulletin boards or internet sites, print it in newspapers, use flyers, or personally invite men to participate.

3. Require a written response from potential members, describing
    themselves and why they want to be part of the group. After review-
    ing requests to join the group, meet with each man in a face-to-face
    interview in order to determine if he is an appropriate candidate for
    your group. Close the recruitment once you have selected 10 to 12
    men.

4. With your group of selected men, proceed through the first eight
    meetings, following the agendas in this manual. These first eight
    meetings are designed to both bond the group and to learn important
    communication skills that will be used throughout the life of the
    group.

5. After the eight initial meetings are completed, the group will de-
    termine how it should evolve. It may decide to establish goals, or
    to create a vision or mission for the group. What will bring the
    most satisfaction to the group members? This will be your group.
    It should be fun, challenging, and forever a source of strength and
    rejuvenation.

Deciding if Being Part of a Men's Group Is Worth It

Only you can decide; but here are some of the benefits, and here are
some of the costs. Achieving a happier life seems like a big reason for
doing anything. We as men are taught many traits, like duty, sacrifice,
obligation, loyalty, invulnerability, etc. Much of what we are taught is
to be honored, and some is to be questioned. But happiness - isn't that
for boys, not men? We often feel that we need to disguise a quest for
happiness as a quest for "growth" or "fulfillment." To admit to wanting
to be happier sounds to many like a boy wanting to go to Disney World.
Involvement in my men's group increases my participation and joy in
living and that increases my happiness. For me that makes the effort
worth it.

While participating in typical social organizations, business and community projects also provides me with joy, they don't easily serve as
vehicles for navigating across the boundaries of acquaintanceship to
authentic kinship. They are bound by social order and polite manners.
In such settings, over sharing, or flatly refusing to share, or demanding
that you speak, or receiving no replies to your comments appears rude

and will not be abided. Yet, when social limitations are dropped in order to facilitate honesty in a men's group, a new level of intimacy can be achieved.

Achieving anything of value has costs. The first and easiest to understand is time. You must be physically present or you will not achieve the benefits. The second is energy. Being open and emotionally accessible can be both invigorating and exhausting. I compare it to exercising. A heavy workout is exhausting, yet paradoxically it is invigorating. The long term benefits from physical exercise have been well documented. I believe the same can be said for emotional exercise. The long term benefits from emotional exercise include a stronger character, healthier personality and longer life. The key phrase here is long term. If you quit either physical or emotional exercise after two weeks, you gain nothing.

If you have decided it is worth proceeding and if you are the initial organizer, you will need to first identify the commonalities you want the men in the group to share. Then you must find men with these interests and the characteristics. Finally and most importantly, you must discover how to bond the men together into an intimate, safe, and supportive group. If you are not the initial organizer, you are still responsible for the organization and success of the group. You should read though every chapter and understand what happens at each step of the process. You must decide as you read if you will be committed to this group, how you can help with this organizing effort, or if you would rather form a different group. Only by understanding the formation of the group can you understand its character and aid its success.

Joining an Existing Group

If you are considering joining a group that has been established for a long time, read with special attention *Chapter 14: Men Exiting - Men Joining*. You will soon learn that you are not joining an existing group but rather a group that is reforming with you and each man as a new member of equal standing. You are integral to the group's new formation and you must take the same ownership as does each other member of the group.

Chapter 3:
Shaping an Intentional Community

When one of the men first called our group an intentional community, I had a momentary negative reaction. It was as if being "intentional" somehow meant the group was artificial or made up. And indeed, in some ways it is made up, but it is not artificial. I do woodworking for a hobby, so I will use a tool metaphor here. When cutting wood, I would always grab a stick out of the trash to use as a tool for pushing it into the blade of my power table saw. It works, sort of. One day I saw a tool designed by a friend just for that task. It worked better, was safer, and made the work easier. We both had a tool. His was an intentionally designed tool; mine was not. The next day, I intentionally designed and made my own tool to work with my saw.

In the same way, an intentionally designed community functions better than something that you may have stumbled upon or adapted. So let's start designing. The first decision is to identify what commonalities the group will share. We have one already, we are all men. If you are the initial organizer, then you get to create the community you want. I call the man that gets the ball rolling the initial organizer simply because he is the first member of the group. If he has found you, or you have found him, it is most likely that his design for the group is very similar to the one you would have created. I know that because the key elements of the group were communicated to you before you contacted him. If, after reading this book and learning the procedures that he followed, you find that you disagree with what he has done, let him know and start a different group. On the other hand, variations in interest and overlapping commonalties are healthy for the group. Your commonalities need not and will not match on every point with every man in the group. But it is important that you share some commonalties beyond gender, and most important that you share a commitment to the group and the support of each man in the group.

The following are three examples of posters for new groups, each of which have very different commonalities and the groups will be very different in character. Some men will be better suited to one group, others to another. After you examine the descriptions of each group, we will begin the process of determining the character of your group.

JOIN NEW MEN'S GROUP

A new Men's Group is forming in January. The group of ten men will meet weekly to discuss topics of mutual interest, personal issues confronting us and share the passing of our lives. Such groups create deep friendships that are often missing in today's world of impersonal interactions. If you enjoy discussing spiritual, philosophic, social and at times even political topics, then you may want to consider joining. We are looking for men who have some interest in authors like Joseph Campbell, Sam Keen, Robert Bly, Carl Jung or Mircea Eliade. We will be using *The Men's Group Manual* as our organizing guidebook. (See www.MensGroupManual.com) If you are interested send a comprehensive email telling us about yourself and why you want to be part of this group.

Send it to: xxxxxxxxxx@xxxxx.com.

(Poster A)

St. Luke's MEN'S GROUP

In January a new Men's Group is forming at St. Luke's Lutheran Church. The group of ten men will meet every Thursday night from 7:00 to 9:30 p.m. We will be discussing how our faith impacts our lives, personal issues confronting us, and sharing the passing of our lives together. In addition to our weekly meetings, we plan to occasionally do charity work together at homeless shelters, nursing homes and with youth organizations.

If you enjoy discussing spiritual, ethical, social topics from a biblical perspective, then you may want to be part of our group. We will be using *The Men's Group Manual* as our organizing guidebook.

(See www.MensGroupManual.com)

If you are interested send a comprehensive email telling us about yourself and why you want to be part of this group.

Send it to: XXXXXXXXXX@XXXXX.com. **(Poster B)**

DAD'S MEN'S GROUP

A new Men's Group for dads between the ages of 35 to 45 is forming in Hilliard. We will meet once a week, starting in January, without our children to discuss topics of mutual interest, personal issues confronting us, and share the events of our lives. With the obligations of fatherhood it becomes more difficult to have some time for yourself and to make new friends. This group is designed to create opportunities to build a supportive network. We will be using *The Men's Group Manual* as our organizing guidebook.
(See www.MensGroupManual.com)
If you are interested send a comprehensive email telling us about yourself and why you want to be part of this group. Send it to: XXXXXXXXXX@XXXXX.com.

(Poster C)

We are all multi-faceted men with many interests. However, if you are the initial organizer it is imperative that you provide an understanding of the group's general interest or focus as part of the solicitation for group members. You can see that each sample poster describes a very different group. Poster A is very detailed about the authors of interest, and contains a few that are very seldom read by the general public. The men who join this group will share a commonality in intellect but may be very different with regard to employment, age, marital status, sexual orientation, political affiliation, and income. They may be very similar in education, spiritual quest, favorite movies, vocabulary, and a host of other things. Poster B, because it is clearly organizing for a particular church, will share the same faith commitment. In Poster C, fathers in a certain age group live in a named location. Each named element carries with it a whole set of other likelihoods. For example, if you name a suburb from which you are drawing members, the income and education tends to be similar. All three groups are broad enough to create some diversity, and narrow enough to establish a commonality. Whatever words you use to describe your group affects who will reply. Consider if the word "divorced" had been placed in front of fathers in Poster C. Even though the original example did not exclude divorced fathers, adding the requirement would attract men who might not otherwise join and definitely exclude others. Adding both married and divorced widens the attraction.

Determining What to Put in Your Posting

The next four chapters are a series of exercises that will help the initial organizer define the group. In the end you might not use all of them, but now is the time to really think through what you want this group to be. The guidelines for actually writing the post will not occur until Chapter 7, but these exercises will determine the character of the group that you will later describe.

If you have responded to the postings of the initial organizer, please read through this section. You might not need to fill it out, but it will give you an understanding of how and why your group was presented the way it was.

Common Intellectual Interest

Intellectual interests are perhaps the most difficult to define. I have found that a few words will convey the broad interest area while still narrowing the range enough to find men with an explicit common interest. Just as any three points define a plane in geometry, this three point system defines intellectual interests. In my examples I will use three authors, books, or well-known personalities. Look at the sets below and imagine what the men in these groups might be like.

Men interested in the following:

A. Joseph Campbell
Carl Jung
Sam Keen

B. Avatar
Star Wars
The Lord of the Rings

C. Saint Thomas Aquinas
Saint Augustine of Hippo
Pope John Paul II

D. The Happiness Project, by Gretchen Rubin
The Secret, by Rhonda Byrne
Happier, by Tal-Bar-Shaha

E. The Bible
The Koran
The Bhagavad-Gita

You may be familiar with some of the above and don't have a clue about the others. That's why you would fit in better with the ones you recognize. You might not have read them, but you might have heard about them and have some interest. Or, you might be looking at the groups and think that each of them appeals to you in some way. That's because we are multi-faceted in our interests and personalities.

You may also think that different names could be substituted that would more closely parallel your interests. For example, placing the Bible with the Koran and the Bhagavad-Gita defines an interest in comparative religions. Including Joseph Campbell instead of the Bhagavad-Gita indicates a group interested more in mythological discussion of scriptural stories. If the Bible is paired with John Calvin and Immanuel Kant, suddenly its focus shifts to philosophic issues of moral conduct with a bit of traditional Protestant perspective. If the Bible were paired with two contemporary evangelists, that would be something entirely different. Pairing Joseph Campbell with Carl Jung reflects a different direction than when he is paired with Star Wars.

The exercise below will help you to determine your intellectual interests. Create one to three groups of three words. (More if you want.) Note that this list will not include activities such as hiking, bowling, or attending the opera. That will come later. This is a list of the things you like to think and talk about. You may love white water rafting but it is mainly experienced physically. Immanuel Kant is experienced intellectually. Try to make each group connected, the three points defining one plane of interest. If you have broad interests, there is a temptation to include interests from three different groups with no apparent connection. But the goal here is to define the hue and texture of a broad interest area for each word combination, not the breadth of all the interests shared by the group. Do not write "reading," "theater," and "movies." Be specific.

I have used mainly people and books in my examples but feel free to use anything that might be discussed - countries, schools of art, genres of writing, fields of science, periods in history, or others. Think this sentence in your head, "Many of the men have a specific interest in ….

1. _____

_____

_____

2. _____

_____

3.   _____

_____

_____

Common Broad Category Interest

Now I want you to define some big general areas that you are interested
in. For example:

A.   Health
        Food
        Exercise

B.   Vegetarianism
        Environmentalism
        Animal rights

D.   Food
        Wine
        Travel

E.   Parenting
        Education
        Sports

F.   Human Rights
        Politics
        Healthcare

Again these groupings define a direction. Notice that food is mentioned
in two of the example groupings, yet by reading the other interest categories in each group you can easily understand that men who pair it
with wine and travel are different from men who pair it with health and

exercise. Again, think this sentence in your head, "Many of the men have a broad interest in ….

1. _____

_____

_____

2. _____

_____

_____

Common Activity Interest

Now we are going to do the same thing again, this time with activities. Most men's groups tend to be devoted to discussions. But sometimes, your group may decide to do things together, with or without the men's partners or families. However, you may want a group that is mainly an activity-based group. Many are a bit of both. For example, you might meet each week to talk, but go hiking or canoeing a few times each summer.

List six activities you like to do, or would like to try doing with other men, in two groups of three words. They might be very physical like white water rafting, or more sedate like attending movies or concerts, or participatory like cooking or drumming. Remember, you might never have done these things before, but you think they would be fun to try.

Some examples might be:

A.   Hiking
        Camping
        Hunting

B   Skeet Shooting
         Guns
         Hunting

C.   Drumming
         Native American Pow-wows
         Sweat lodges

D.   Attending the symphony
         Attending chamber music concerts
         Attending the opera

Notice again my first two examples both include hunting, but are nu-
anced such that they might describe two different groups of men. In example D had I just said music, a guy might assume it was Rock 'n Roll,
Blues, and Grunge, because that is what music is to many of us. The
group described in example D is very different from groups that could
be defined by three other kinds of music. If, on the other hand, you do
really want to find men who want to explore all music inclusively, then
say, Rap, Classical, and County. (Later when you are actually writing
it, you might change it to read "All music from …to…)

Think of the sentence, "Some of the men in our group enjoy …"

1.   _____

_____

_____

2.   _____

_____

_____

If you responded to a posting and you're not familiar with any of the
interests listed, take some time right now to do a little research. The
primary focus of the group is not going to be an intense study of these

subjects, as would be expected in a seminar, professional guild, or specialized interest club, but it is meant more to define the curiosities of the men attracted to this group. For example, if you saw that every one of the authors listed are current evangelicals and evangelicalism is aligned with your general belief system, then even if you hadn't read any of their works, and even if they are never discussed in the group, you would still relate to the other men's perspectives and insights. On the other hand, if you are currently exploring Buddhism and want to discuss your evolving understanding of this philosophy with others who may be interested in hearing and supporting your exploration, then you may want to join a group that mentioned several spiritual paths or Buddhism specifically, rather than seeking out an evangelical group.

Wikipedia is a great resource for learning the basic ideas of authors or philosophers, and other interests mentioned on a post. You might find that you would like to learn more, and that while you haven't had the opportunity previously to learn about these topics, you are attracted to the idea of doing so.

A functioning group is not a group that directs men in any predetermined course of thought, or limits a man from exploring new interests, but rather one that celebrates our ability to continuously grow and change throughout our lives. How many points of commonality must members of the group have? I think at least one. A few more are better. The more commonalties you have starting out, the greater your chances are for a successfully bonded group, a group that will be able to support the many changes each man may undergo over the years. Chances are that you will not find a single man in the group that shares all the same interests. That's great. With a variety of interests that only occasionally overlap, discussions will be far more dynamic over the years.

NOTE: If you are responding to a posting because you are interested in a men's group, but after researching find that you are repulsed by every author and/or interest listed, it is time for you to be the initial organizer of a new group. The good news is, joining or starting a group takes the same commitment, and the work is only slightly more for the initial organizer. Read on and you can form a group that will better suit your needs and interests.

Chapter 4:
Optional Commonalities

Faith

If you are forming a faith-based community of men, this will be the single most important commonality. But even within a faith-based community, you may want to distinguish your group based on other factors. For example, your group could be a group described as:

Men from the church who have struggled with alcohol

Men from the church trying to be better fathers/husbands

Men caring for aging parents

Men with an interest in community service

Men newly retired

Men striving to live a biblically-based life

Men interested in conservation

If you are a member of a large church, multiple men's groups are better. Remember to keep each group around ten.

Should the clergy be a part of these groups? I advise not. The role of the clergy within the church generally is a role as leader, counselor, or teacher. Separating his role as a member of the clergy from that of a member in the group could prove difficult. The groups need to be formed by equals. They need to be owned by the members. A church leader added to the mix could appear to have more responsibilities and authority. I recommend that church ministers join or create men's groups that have no members from their own church in them; perhaps with other male clergy, either of the same or different faiths. That way he is free to be himself rather than playing his role, and the other men in his group will be able to authentically react to him.

Will this group be formed around my Faith or Religion?

_____ Yes

_____ No

If yes, which Faith or Religion?

Shared Past Crises

Rather than shared interests or activities commonality, some men's groups are based on shared crisis. These groups are designed to meet specific needs of the men. Men in these groups would not have chosen to be a part of the group, but because a negative event or condition occurred, they realize that they need the support of other men to deal with their situation. Men in these groups might include victims of disease, crime, war, fathers and husbands of victims, grief groups, and men dealing with weight, alcohol or drug issues. A self-initiated group is not equipped to deal with an ongoing crisis. Only professionals in various fields are trained to handle these. However, after professional treatment or intervention is completed, men may want to form relationships with other men who have overcome the same difficulty. While there are many well-established groups already organized that deal with these issues, if there are none that meet your needs and you are qualified to start such a group, you may find some of the information in this book to be useful; but never attempt to start any type of crisis treatment or crises support group for which you are not qualified. This book is not intended to be a manual for any psychological treatment or crisis management group.

Fill in the Following

Will this group be formed around common crisis that has been treated and overcome?

____Yes

____No

If yes, what is the focus?

___

Age

Organizations that are inter-generational are not very common in the twenty-first century. But let's compare today's social structure with that of a hundred or even fifty years ago. Back then, a 16-year-old Jewish youth growing up in New York City would have had a great deal in common and would have identified himself with his older brothers, his father, his uncles, and even his grandfather more than he would have identified himself with a 16-year-old Hindu youth in India. Then, youths and adults in the same ethnic group would have dressed alike, read the same books, enjoyed the same music, known the same stories, and believed in the same spiritual pathways as the men in their family and community had for millennia.

Today, the two 16-year-olds, even if one is a Hindu in India and the other a Jew in New York, are probably wearing the same T-shirt from Abercrombie & Fitch, listening to the same music, watching the same "YouTube" clips, playing the same video games, and even reading the same books. Both would be very unlikely to be wearing the same clothing or engaging in the same activities as their older brothers, father, uncles, or grandfather. We no longer get our cultural values from vertically-integrated organizations; we get them from horizontally-structured institutions. All 16-year-olds worldwide are instructed to wear the same clothing by an effectively run global marking effort. Fifty to a hundred years ago, the young Jewish man would have dressed distinctively, similar to this father, and the Indian youth would have dressed like his father. Today, a 16-year-old girl is less likely to wear what her

12-year-old sister is wearing. Sixty-five-year-olds in retirement villages
will not permit a young couple to move in, and if grandparents assume
custody of grandchild, the neighborhood association will force them to
move out.

While I may have exaggerated the point a bit, the contrast in the change
from a vertically-structured culture to a horizontal one is undeniable.
In the broader economic world, such a structure permits the effective
marketing to each layer of a modern world culture. I'm not making a
value judgment. I'm just conveying what economists and marketers
know about our current cultural behavior.

Your men's group is an intentional community. You can decide what
you want it to be. Limiting the ages of potential members as shown in
Poster C, your group will mimic the general culture, and therefore may
appear to be more accessible to men comfortable with social norms.
The men joining the group will bond more rapidly. Some men, particularly men under 40, will feel uncomfortable sharing themselves with
men their father's age, and therefore will avoid vertically-integrated
groups. However, other young men hunger for an opportunity to talk
openly with men who have walked the path that they are now venturing
on. An age vertically-integrated group provides men of every age an
opportunity to see their lives in the larger context of the male life cycle.
Younger men realize they don't suddenly become some strange alien
being when they pass fifty. Older men tend to recognize the challenges
confronting younger men, and can assure them that nearly every man
has confronted the same conflicts; they may even have insights that will
help the younger man in his course. Such mentoring was once common
in nearly every culture but has become increasingly rare today. The
younger men will be able to see the older men in ways that will make
their futures less scary and better illuminated. There are treasures to be
had in vertically-integrated groups, but there are also hurdles that may
be difficult to overcome. When we formed our group over twenty years
ago, we did not include any age restrictions. We wanted an age spread.
However, all of the men turned out to be around forty. Each time we
have opened the group for new members, most of the men have been
around that same age. Our group now has an age span from a man in
his thirties to a man in his seventies. It is the best group we have ever
had. We have truly achieved the re-establishment of the men's hut in
our contemporary Ohio community. But even if you want it, it may take
time to get it. Don't give up.

This is one that simply calls for a decision. Will we accept men from a wide range of ages, or will we not?

____ Any Age

____ Only Ages ____ to ____

Political Views

The world has become fairly tolerant of various points of view in a lot of areas; however, politics is another story. You have three choices here. First, restrict the group to capital letter Liberals. Second, restrict the group to capital letter Conservatives. Third, tolerate everyone's views. The reality is that partisans on both ends of the political spectrum often have difficulty seeing another man as a man and not an enemy. Men cannot bond if they are emotionally tied to a dogmatic belief system that cannot accept that a man with another point of view has value, is moral, has the ability to love, and cares about his fellow man. Only if men can accept the value of the person, apart from his proposed solutions to human problems, can solutions be debated. Only when the effectiveness of a solution can be objectively deliberated can we say that we have tolerance. If you cannot envision yourself bonding with and being open and defenseless with a man who holds different political views, then honestly make a decision to discriminate on political grounds. It would be a travesty to invite a man into a community that claims to be open if there are areas where it is not. Being part of a successful men's group means above all else being honest. Honesty starts with you. If one of the commonalities that you want for your group is a particular political persuasion, then say so.

On the other hand, sharing political perspectives openly while still being able to accept the value of the man and understand the structure of his position does open one's mind to thinking in ways that men do not experience if they shutter themselves in rooms with like-thinking, self-assured men. If you decide that you will accept all men regardless of political views, then you have an obligation to protect each man from onslaughts of partisan attacks and to keep conversations civil. This can be particularly difficult in groups where there is an imbalance, or where extreme positions are held steadfastly. The good news is if you choose not to discriminate, you will most likely end up with a lot of independents and moderates. After all, even with all the blue and red maps these days, moderates and independents are by far more common than extremists.

___ Open to all political affiliations

___ Must be on the Left

___ Must be on the Right

___ Open to true Independents only

Sexual Orientation

Men often ask if the group is open to gay men. It might be asked because the man asking it is gay, because the man does not want to be part of a group that would discriminate against other men who are gay, or because the man doesn't want to be part of a group with gay men.

While the media would have you believe that many men would refuse to join a group if it were open to gay men, in my many years of involvement with men's groups I have never been told by any man that they would not join if gays were permitted. However, again, it's your group; you can decide. You can also decide that you want only gay men. Whichever position you choose, you will find men in agreement.

In designing your intentional community, you must be honest and clearly communicate what the intentions are. If you are restricting the group to strictly heterosexual men, then somewhere in your post you might include the word "straight." If you are restricting your group to strictly homosexual men, then include the word "gay." If you're non-discriminating, simply say nothing. You might still get questions, so be prepared with your reply.

Here is my advice regarding participation of gay partners. This guideline imposes the same restriction on everyone in the group and protects the equality of each member. No group should include partners. Straight men do not bring their spouses, so neither should gay men. This restriction may at first seem a bit odd, but remember that in the group every man must be free to express himself without consequences outside the group. If couples were permitted in the group, this would be an unequal relationship. The heterosexual men are there unsupported by their mate. If a gay couple was present and one man wanted to say that he is thinking about ending the relationship and wants to talk it through, he could not do it with the other man there. What works best is that every man is equal and no man brings his partner. If a relationship does form in the group, they and the group will have to decide which man leaves or whether both men should leave. The group is not set up for partnership counseling if difficulties develop, nor would it be fair to put the men in a position where they might be expected to take sides.

___ Open to all men

___ Open only to heterosexual men

___ Open only to gay men

___ Other options or requirements _____

Ethnicity

The law does not prevent private clubs and churches from discriminating based on race or ethnicity. You may have a group that is all Black, White, Asian, Native American or any other requirement you elect to impose. My personal advice is that, by limiting membership on the basis of race, you are losing a richness that the group might otherwise have. But I cannot deny that race is a basis for commonality. There are many professional groups restricted to one ethnicity or another. While a hundred years ago many clubs and organization were restricted to white men only, today it is more common for groups to be restricted to black men only, Native Americans only, and so on. Many of these groups have formed in reaction to our nation's dysfunctional history, and I do understand the constructive motivation for them. If your intent is to racially restrict your group, do so in the posting. It can be done by adding words like "African American," "Black," "European Heritage," "Sons of Israel," " Sons of Ireland," "Germanic Ancestry," etc.

___ Open to all men

___ Open only to men who are of _____ ancestry.

Do You Really Need Commonalities?

If you're thinking, "But I want a really diverse group," and have come to the conclusion that you don't care what the group's interest profile is, that it is not necessary for you to share any commonality, or that all that is required is commitment, then please reread this section. Do you really think that a group of men made up of a Ku Klux Klan member, a gay Jewish man, a fundamentalist African-American, a right wing philosophy professor, a guy who only watches sports, a guy who never read a book in his life, a Dungeons and Dragons enthusiast, a left wing soap opera fan, an avid hunter, a PETA member, and a French chef would be a group where every man felt safe, open and valued? Such a group, I will admit, would be an exciting forum for debate. But it does not have a solid foundation for building an intentional community of men that are bonded. Unless they are all Buckeye football fans or have some other fanatical common ground, it will fail. I realize that my example is extreme, but when men cannot find any way that they are similar, bonding is difficult. Why dramatically increase your chance of failure? Find at least one commonality to build on, and it might work. Find the right mix of similarities and differences, and you can easily form into a bonded group with enough diversity to challenge each other and grow.

It is imperative that you give men considering this group an accurate idea of who you are. A total lack of commonality will make it difficult for your group to bond. The more similar the men are in your group in terms of values and world view, the easier it will be for the group to bond. Think the character of your group through and decide what you would like it to be, and be forthright.

Chapter 5:
Meeting Logistics

Finding a Location to Meet

If your group is organized through a church, health club, or school, you may already have a place to hold meetings. Otherwise, here are some considerations. If the group is made up of men who don't know each other, then you might want to consider using a neutral location. Many public libraries, city park systems, YMCAs, schools, churches, or other community organizations have meeting rooms that are available free of charge. You might need to have a name for your group to reserve a room, so make one up before you ask. Some larger cities and libraries permit organizations registered with them to reserve rooms on-line. Some restaurants also have meeting rooms; they generally require that you buy food and drinks. Sometimes, men who operate their own business may have a board room, conference room, or waiting room available.

Less neutral, but perhaps more convenient, are homes. The meetings are confidential, so privacy is a must. If you're meeting and other people are at home (partners or children), you need to make sure that the men feel safe and that privacy is preserved. Some groups rotate meetings between the member's homes. But some men cannot make their homes available. (Perhaps an elderly parent lives with them, or they have a lot of children and a small home or apartment.) Or, meetings might be rotated only between the homes of a few of the men. Perhaps only one man has a great basement recreation room, and he and his family are willing to have it used every week. That will work provided that the leadership for each meeting rotates, and that he and the group doesn't feel that it is his group because they meet at his home. The most important advice is, make absolutely sure that the space is available. Nothing will shake up your first meeting faster than announcing that you don't have a place to meet. Before you start, make sure that you have a location for the first eight meetings.

Frequency

Time is the biggest unavoidable cost of being in a men's group. You have two choices here, once a week or once every two weeks, but once a week appears to be the magic number. For thousands of years, the most successful communities have met at least once a week. I think that's why churches have evolved this custom. There is no other way to have a closely-bonded group than spending time bonding. Meeting once a week means that your men's group is going to be an integral and important part of your life. This is a true commitment.

I have known groups that meet every other week. They tend to fall apart more often. If a man misses one meeting, it will be a month before you see him again. If a man misses two meetings in a row, six weeks will have passed, and he is much more likely to drift out of the group. These longer intervals are not as damaging after the group has bonded. Twelve times a year will not be worthwhile, so it is not worth your time trying something that will not succeed.

Although groups that meet every other week tend to fall apart, a few don't. What's the difference? The successful ones started out meeting every week, sometimes for years, and then evolved into meeting every two weeks. The bonds were already tightly formed and the strain of two-week intervals could be overcome. I would suggest that if you are planning on being an every-other-week group, you meet every week for at least the first six months. All logistical arrangements, including the number of times you meet, are always open to change by consensus.

Some groups change their schedule at different times during the year. For example, they meet every week, but during the summer become an every-other-week group. It works because they know they will return to their routine in the fall. (It feels a bit like college, when everyone is off on various adventures and then they "get back to business" in the fall.) Some also skip meetings around the holidays.

___ Weekly

___ Weekly for the first ____ months, then every other week

___ Every other week

When and for How Long

You can decide the time and day with the other men who will be joining the group or you can decide by yourself now. If you will be including the input of the other men, then in Chapter 9, The Face to Face, you will find a practical way to do so. If you have already decided when the group will meet, put it on the poster, as in Poster B. If they can't meet then, they won't reply. However, a decision must be made before your first meeting as to which day you will meet and for how long. The meeting day can and probably will change over the years as the men are faced with ever-changing obligations and schedule conflicts.

Most groups meet in the evening, but other times may work better for your group. The time block needed runs from 1.5 hours to 2.5 hours. The longer time is better. If ten men are meeting for only 1.5 hours, each man is speaking for less than eight minutes total during each meeting. That's not much time to comfortably communicate the events affecting him and his feelings about them. If you absolutely need to have meetings shorter than 2.5 hours, then make the group smaller, six or seven men. But remember, a group that size is not optimal, and tends to fail more frequently.

Our meeting time is 7:30 pm to 10:00pm. For you, right after work might be better, or even before work or a long lunch. Deciding to hold meetings during the day will of course limit who can join and should be noted on the poster. Men with fewer daytime commitments will have more flexibility, but most men will not be able to participate.

Chapter 6:
Membership

There are millions of men, but you only want ten. Again, nine to eleven is the optimal number. Five is the bare minimum and twelve is big. Despite everything you do, you might still have some drop-outs. So starting with twelve is often a good idea. If everyone stays, or someone leaves, you are still in the size range.

New or Existing Friends

All the men in the world can be placed in two categories

One - Men you don't know
Two - Men you know

So from which group will you draw the members?

Men You Don't Know

Earlier I wrote about a stage in my life where I had many associates, all with their own agendas. The men I knew from work were superiors or subordinates. The other men I knew were half of a couple, relatives, or fellow members of an organization, many of which functioned like work situations. I had friends from high school and college years, but they were miles away. I decided that I wanted to have friends with whom I had no other associations. The advantage of this would be that I would have nine new friends that shared common interests and who also wanted to be part of a men's group. I would not have to decide if they were joining the group because they wanted to please me, network with me, or simply lacked the will power to refuse. Pursuing this path, I became immediately aware that I would have to select very carefully.

This was before the age of the internet. I started the same way that I've instructed you, by first deciding what kind of men I wanted. Then I designed a letter-sized poster with tear-offs. I wanted the process to be somewhat self-selecting in order to narrow the final choices.

During my career, I had the opportunity to select new employees at our firm many times. I knew that if I put a few hurdles up before we got to an interview, the men who would not make good members of the group would not even make it that far. This may sound callous, but I wanted men who would follow through. So on the posting I asked each man who was interested in joining to write a letter telling me about himself and why he wanted to join. I rented a post office box for this purpose. No phone number was given.

I knew it would be difficult. First, it takes courage to write to a blind mailbox, exposing yourself and your desire for deep friendships. That assured me these men had heart, they were able to recognize their desire for the group, and they had enough aggressiveness to work for what they wanted. Second, it told me that they were willing to give time and effort. Third, reading their letters gave me insight into their thinking, what they were curious about, how organized their thinking was, and what their interests were. While I didn't mention it on the poster, they also had to be smart enough to give me contact information. In most cases, I received a phone number so I could contact them.

If I had given them a phone number, I would have gotten hundreds of calls, and most would not have amounted to anything. Or I might have been so impressed by their phone voice and presence that I would have chosen badly. Each of the 10 posters that were put up had ten tear-offs. When the last tear-off was gone, all of the vital information was still available printed on the poster. When we took down the posters, all of the tear-offs were gone. I knew that more than 100 men had been interested, but I only received 15 well-written letters.

I then proceeded to the next step of the selection process, the face-to-face interviews with the men that gave a clear indication in their letters that they would be a valuable group member.

Men You Know

You may want to assemble your group with men you know. You will have some advantages and some disadvantages. First, you will likely have something in common already. You may like these guys and simply want to set up the group so that you will have a specific time to meet and a method by which you can grow closer. In assembling this group, there must be a level of equal power. For example, groups that will not work include: the boss and all the guys who work for him; a probation officer and the men that he is in charge of; a college teacher and his students; or a salesman and his customers. If any man in the group has the power to affect another man outside the group, then it will not work. If there is a networking advantage, either financially, socially, or politically for any man to join the group, then it will not work.

Using one of the examples, a group of grad students that are not competing for grades could work. Adding their graduate advisor would not work. If there is competition between the students in the group for scholarships, grades, or internships, the possibility for complete openness is gone. How about students from different departments? Bingo, a winner! They are not competing, but are all connected by the same joys, defeats, fears, and hopes of their pursuits. There is an emotional and intellectual commonality, but no motivation for manipulation.

The members of your health club might work. You share the commonality to work out, have proximity to the club, may have similar schedules, and most likely similar incomes. Now if you can invite men with whom you don't have other connections or for whom networking would not be a primary motive, it should work.

What about fathers at your child's school or childcare center? You might have met them through volunteering or other school-related events, or maybe just by waiting to pick up the kids at the preschool. Commonality is present; you've got kids - that's a big commonality. It could work.

Church men's groups are another possibility. Today participation in many churches has no financial or social implications. This wasn't always the case. Some churches are still filled with internal politics, networking, and maneuvering for social and economic position; others are sincere communities of believers. Only you can decide if your church is the right place to find your members, as in sample Poster B. The commonality is that you all espouse some commonality of belief.

Fellow military men you know, either veterans or currently serving, or husbands of military women, present great opportunities to form a group if you deal with issues of rank.

Men from your neighborhood or suburb generally have a lot in common in terms of values, income, and education. But unless you live in a company town, you are unconnected in many other ways.

If you put some thought into it, you will be able to think up endless opportunities for assembling a team of men. I even heard of one group made up of men who knew each other because their wives were very involved in the women's liberation movement. They say that their common connection was being married to strong women. The number one rule here is: do not create a mix of men where what happens in the group could have consequences outside the group.

_____   The group will be made up of men who do not know each other. I will draw these men from (my neighborhood, city wide, other)

_____   The group will be made up of men that I already know. (Make a list.)

_____   The group will be made up of a combination of men I know and don't know.

Chapter 7:
Finding Your Members

The Process

1. Design and write your post.

2. Post the information at locations in your area and on the internet.

3. Read the requests to join and follow-up with more information, or if it is obvious that they are not a viable candidate, let them know.

4. Set up a face-to-face meeting with each man.

5. Decide whom to invite and whom to decline. Inform each man of your decision.

6. Gather together for your first meeting.

It sounds simple, but there can be many traps and unseen pitfalls along the way. This manual will guide you through most of them. If you saw the post and responded to it, please read this chapter, too. It is important that you know why the initial organizer proceeded as he did.

Where to Receive Your Inquiries

The first task is to set up a place to receive inquiries. As I said earlier, I do not recommend giving a phone number. First, do you really want your phone number floating out there? And second, phoning is too easy. A serious candidate should be willing to write. In the past, I have suggested renting a post office box for a month or two. It's inexpensive and provides anonymity for you. To do so, you must provide a location address to the post office, and they need to verify it. When they do so, you will get your box. It takes about a week or two. Many of the UPS and other delivery services also have boxes to rent. I would put the box in some kind of a name. Ours was simply called The Columbus Men's Group. Or, if you want to get more creative, make up a name for your group

The other option is an email address. Using an email address does self-select men who are computer literate. You could do both snail mail and email, if it is important to you to open the group to men who might not have access to a computer. But, my advice is to use email; it will make future communication easier, too. Set up the email account. I like Gmail, but other free emails that I know of include Hotmail and Yahoo. I think they all work about the same, and at present they are all free. The one caveat that I would add is to use a name that is clearly identifiable with a men's group. For example, we used ColumbusMensGroup@ gmail.com (Columbus Men's Group). It's easy to remember and it's clear what it is. You might want to do the same with your town. If someone has beaten you to the name you want, just add the word "New" or some numbers. One person needs to be in charge of the mailbox. If you are the initial organizer, that's you.

Writing Your Message

Writing a clear message is the most important step. More than anything else you do, it will affect the success or failure of your group.

First, look again at the sample posters that I have included in Chapter 3, and on the website at www.MensGroupManual.com. Then return to the lists that you made in the earlier chapters. Circle the words that you wrote in each of the exercises that you think will attract the kind of men you want. If you think some of the exercises don't really apply, don't use any of the words from it. Then think about what implications each word has, and what limiting factors or broadening factors might be triggered by adding specific words to your description. You might, for example, use all three items in a grouping on one list but deicide to only use one word from another list. You might decide to add other words you hadn't thought of when you did the exercises but now find that you need to describe your group. If you're drawing from a small pool of men, such as the fathers at your child's preschool, then you may be better off with broader topics or even focusing on just one commonalty such as "dads." You will already have a lot in common having chosen the same preschool. On the other hand, if you are drawing ten men from a pool of a million or more, as in a citywide group, then you can be more selective. You can mix from broad and narrowed categories the interests and commonalities that you think best describe your group.

The copy should be about 150 words but not more than 200 words, better if it is under 150 words. Look at each of the exercises that you completed. As demonstrated in the examples, you do not have to use words from every list; likewise, you can add other information that limits or expands who is invited. You will notice in example Poster B, the time for the meetings is already given because the initial organizer has already determined that this will be the only time available for the first eight meetings.

I strongly advise including a reference to the Men's Group Manual. A potential member can go to the website for more information. You want men who will do a little investigation rather than just jumping in.

Start typing "A new men's group…" and keep going, using the words that describe what you want your group to be, and end by telling interested men where to send an inquiry. Edit and leave it for at least a day. Then read it again and see if it clearly conveys the character of the group and whether anything is missing.

Laying Out Your Post

I recommend using the words MEN'S GROUP in big bold letters. That way, it's clear what you are. If your group is going to be limited by a particular factor, also put that on top as in Poster C, "Men's Group for Fathers." A photo, logo, or drawing can help to catch the eye. There are lots of stock background posters, including the ones used in this publication, at the website www.MensGroupManual.com, under the Sharing Information tab. As an owner of this manual you are free to use them for the purpose of recruiting men for a local men's group. The text boxes are empty so you can add your own copy. On some of the posters, the headline is also removed. If you are drawing members from a particular church or location, you can edit that information as needed.

Your main text should be placed at the bottom. If you print the poster on light card stock and then reprint the contact information on regular paper, cut it and staple a stack of 7 to 10 over the text as a tear-off so men can easily take the information. (After the tear-offs are gone, men can still copy down the important items like the address.) As a hint, printing the poster and the tear offs on a light tan stock gives them a bit more interest; the graphics look better and they are still inexpensive to produce.

If you're drawing your group from a specific organization like your church, children's preschool, health club, or from men you know, then a stack of single sheet flyers may be better. They can be set at the front desk or personally handed out.

Placing Your Paper Post

If you are asking men that you don't know, where you post will be very important. On the other hand, if you know everyone that you are asking to join, then you will not need to post at all. In either case, I suggest that you still write your post. Even if you have known the man for twenty years, give him a copy of the post. It is important that he understands what the focus of the group is.

All three types of posts - posters, internet, and newspaper - should contain the same information. The letter-sized poster with tear-offs should be posted on community bulletin boards. Even with the internet, some of the best men for your group will respond to a physical letter-sized poster on an old-fashioned bulletin board. For one thing, their placement can be more targeted to specific demographics. For example, if you want to reach men who read a lot, bookstores work well. However, all bookstores are not the same; some are focused on Spiritual/New Age material, others on Christian literature, and still others on general writings. We have received some of the best replies from coffee house, library, and bookstore boards. But these are not the only places. Many hardware stores and lumber yards have bulletin boards. While they are typically filled with men offering construction-related services, they are viewed primarily by men. Barbershops, grocery stores, restaurants, churches, cultural/recreation centers, health clubs, and schools of various kinds also might have boards.

Since men that share common interests often frequent the same places, make a list of bulletin boards that you notice. When making your list, also notice if there is a requirement for approval before tacking up your poster. A few locations require that the management stamp the posting. When you do post, remember to bring push pins. Write the dates when you want the post to be displayed on your poster, and generally it will be left up until the end date. Otherwise, someone might take it down when the tear-offs are gone.

I recommend that in order to be sure to get plenty of responses you put up 15 to 20 posters. If you get the first five posters up early, let's say 6 to 8 weeks before the first meeting, then you can ask the first three or four men that you interview if they will help you by each putting up five more posters. Together you can decide the best locations. Tell them where you put yours, and make sure they commit to telling you where they put up theirs. If they are not willing to do the work or take the responsibility, they will not be good members. If they say that they will but never get to it, or they never send you the list of where they have put them up, ask. If it becomes obvious that they are not willing to take ownership, or to carry some of the load, confront the situation and suggest that the group carries too much responsibility for them to handle. You are better off losing them now than in three weeks. If they help you, if they take ownership and follow through, you have begun to build the trust that is essential for the group to succeed.

It may be difficult for a man to approach a manager of a store or a librarian and ask if he can put up a poster of this kind. He may fear that he might be asked about it and won't know what to say. (If a man isn't strong enough to meet this challenge, he will not be capable of assuming ownership responsibilities for the group.) The very first poster I ever put up was at the Columbus Public Library's Main Branch. I checked the board and saw many postings for various kinds of groups and book clubs. I noticed that posting required approval. I took my poster to the desk, nearly shaking in my wing-tipped shoes. I was coming from work at a very conservative 1980's architecture firm. I was dressed in a blue suit. The woman looked at it and said, "I don't think we can approve this."

I asked why and she said, "Well it appears that it is for men only."

I said, "That's true, as it is a men's group."

"Well," she replied, "Our policy is that we don't permit discriminatory postings."

I said, "You have a lot of them out there, let me show you." She jumped up and we went to the board where I pointed out three postings for women's groups.

She replied, "That's different, those are women's groups." I asked to talk to the head librarian. She took the poster with her; the two returned talking and looking at the poster. The head librarian, a woman, asked me several perfunctory questions about the group and then said that they decided that they could approve it. I asked her if she had a moment because I had a real concern about the computer card catalog that the library had installed. We walked to a bank of three monitors. I typed in "Women's Rights" on the first, and 247 titles came up. Then I stepped to the next monitor and typed in "Men's Rights." The screen read "Closest match - Metaphase." I smiled, shrugged my shoulders and said, "Just asking." She smiled and appeared a little embarrassed, and we both laughed. She did go on to say that they get their listings from the Library of Congress and they can't change them. But she got my point and would send it in as feedback to the service provider.

The rest of the postings were much less eventful.

Placing Your Electronic Post on the Internet

One of the locations to post on the Internet is Craig's List. You should remove the email address from your copy and instead say, "Reply to this posting." Craig's List will forward your replies to the group's email address for you. Type in www.craigslist.org and it will take you to a page with counties, states and cities. Find your city, or whatever is closest to you. It will take you to listings. Find Community/Groups. Find the post menu and attempt the post. You will be asked to set up an account for posting in Community/Groups. Use the group's email account to set this up. Because it is a Community Group they will further want to make sure that you are legitimate, so they will ask for a phone number. They call, giving you a code to activate your account. Another location you might check out on Craig's List is Community/Local News, but you may need to do a bit of a rewrite. In the news article post, direct interested men to the posting under Community/Groups.

Do a few web searches. Many communities, local organizations, churches, and others have sites where you can post. The better ones have moderators to whom you submit a post and they decide whether and how to post it.

Also, look on our website under the Sharing Information tab at www. MensGroupManual.com to see how you can post your contact information on our site.

Using Newspapers and Neighborhood Shoppers

Most local newspapers have a community section that prints items free of charge. You will need to provide the paper with your name, contact information, and so forth. Some ask that you include a phone number in the article, but don't. You do not want to be getting a bunch of calls. The men who want to join must make the effort to write. If you can't use your email or post office box, just say no thanks.

Removing the Post

Getting a request to join the group after it has formed can be emotionally difficult. It may be hard for the man making the request, too. To lessen the number of such requests, take down all postings as soon as your group is full, rather than waiting for the staff to remove them or the time to expire. The electronic posts can be removed very easily from most sites; the posters take some effort, but you need to do it. Newspaper notices are the least flexible, and you may not be able to stop them. Consider this when asking about run times.

Using Verbal Invitation

If you already know all the men for the group that you want to form, then your task is simple. Tell them that you are interested in starting a men's group, and tell them a bit about what you see as the common interests of the group. Mention this manual as the guide for forming the group and leading the group through the first eight meetings. Give them a copy of your post, and then ask them to let you know by a specific date if they want to be considered for the group. Give them a deadline. Say something like, "Why don't you get the book, or at least check out the website and then if you're interested we will talk about it over coffee.

But I need to know by…" Even if you have decided that you will only invite existing friends or members of a specific organization such as church members, I suggest that you still design a written flyer. While your flyer might be more informal than the one for a broader call, it will still be a necessary informational tool. If he decides he isn't interested, if he doesn't call you to schedule a time for coffee, drop it and move on. If after your group has formed he begins to show interest and asks to join, just let him know that your group has formed and it's closed. Reassure him that it is wonderful that he is interested, and tell him that if he forms his own group, the two groups can do outings together. If he doesn't have the commitment to be an initial organizer, he wouldn't have been a fully participating member anyway. Think of it this way, you have now given him the opportunity to form a group that another ten men can be part of.

Chapter 8:
Responding to Replies

Tracking Prospects

The next steps are replying to the inquiries, meeting potential candidates face-to-face, and making the final selections. It can be challenging to keep track of meetings with nine or more men that you haven't met and have no idea what they look like. Set up a way to track your inquiries. This can be as simple as making a list or an Excel spreadsheet. The information to include is:

Name:

Email:

Phone:

Did he provide some information about himself and why he wanted to join?

When is the face-to-face?

Where is the face-to-face?

Selected as a member?

Is he willing to help you?

What have you asked him to do?

Does he know where and when the first meeting is?

It can be very helpful to print out all emails related to each man and keep them together so that you can take them with you for the face-to-face.

Replies

Replies to Men Who Have Sent a Proper Request

Write a draft of your reply before you get your first contact. But be ready to alter it to address the questions that each man might have. After you have decided that the man has given you enough information about himself and why he wants to join, reply. He will also likely be testing you a bit too, so if you don't reply promptly and directly to his concerns, he might well question your commitment and decide on a better group. He may also need to protect himself a bit. Don't expect him to provide a home address; maybe he will only provide a first name. If using email, on the first reply he may not provide a phone number. If he is responding to a post office box, he needs to give you some way to contact him. Below is a sample reply. It may not be accurate for your group. For example, it assumes that the exact meeting times will be worked out with the members. If you have already advertised the group as meeting at lunch, alter the same reply. Use it as a starting point but feel free to change it as needed.

Sample Reply –A (For Acceptable Request)

(Use the man's name), good to hear from you. Like you, I think that being part of a men's group will be an exciting addition to my life. I have never organized this kind of a group before so I am using Clyde Henry's book, *The Men's Group Manual*, as my guide. In addition to guiding me in organizing the group, it will lead us through the first eight meetings.

We hope to have a good mix of men. Some of the interests that I mentioned in the posting should give you an idea of the group. Other than that, I suspect that topics will range from deep emotional feelings and personal histories, to politics, sex, drugs and Rock 'n Roll, God, and sports. There are no unacceptable topics, but there will be an expectation that every man speaks his true feelings and be open and accepting of the other men's feelings.

Let me try to answer your concerns the best that I can...(Answer any question that he might have asked)

There is no cost to join and no dues to pay. We are just men getting together. We have no agenda other than sharing our lives and our friendship. What we ask, however, is a commitment. We ask you to make a commitment to attend the first eight meetings.

From what you wrote, I think you will be a good member. The next step is to set up a face-to-face meeting. We can meet for coffee before or after work, or have lunch or even breakfast. In the meantime I suggest you get a copy of *The Men's Group Manual* or at least visit the website at www.MensGroupManual.com. By reading through it you will have an understanding of the group and what to expect at each meeting. A good time for me is (name date and time). I live near (name some convenient meeting place) and work near (name another potential meeting place). Let me know in the next few days if that works for you. Otherwise if a different time or place nearer your work is better, let me know.

I'm looking forward to meeting and talking further about the group.

(Your Name)

Wait for a reply; work out a time and location. I suggest giving him a description of what you look like and your cell phone number in case of a last-minute delay. At this point, I think you can trust someone with your phone number, but don't do it if you feel uncomfortable. Typically he will reply with similar information. If you feel comfortable in doing so, you can also give directions to social networking sites like Facebook or LinkedIn.

NOTE: Please don't think I'm suggesting that every man buy a book to push book sales. So that it is not a hardship on anyone to purchase, I have priced the manual near cost. I have put more cash and time into the printing of this book than I ever expect to get back. While a lot of information is on the website for free, everyone in the group really needs to own his own copy of the manual. The printed copy is best because you can write in it and highlight what you find important. This is the only cost to any member. What does it tell you about a man that expects everything to be given to him for free?

Replies to Men Whose Requests are Lacking

Unlike traditional written mail, the internet tends to make correspondence short and spontaneous. Perhaps it's the cost of the first class stamp that makes people more thoughtful. You will get some short and inadequate replies. The most common will be, "Send more information," or "When do you guys meet?" You will also get some very odd ones like, "I'm only interested if this is a nude group." Unless it is really inappropriate, I generally give them one more chance. Send them a form letter and alter it as little as you need to. Below is a draft to start with. You will notice that it has some of the same information as the other reply, so if the man does respond with a proper request, you will need to alter your next communication so that you're not redundant.

Sample Reply – B1 (For Insufficient Request)

(Use the man's name), A Men's group can provide you with a wonderful opportunity to form deep and meaningful relationships. The structure of the group is based on *The Men's Group Manual*, see this website at www.MensGroupManual.com. The group will meet once a week to discuss topics of interest, personal issues confronting us, and other life adventures.

If you are still interested in being considered after checking out the website, send us a comprehensive email, telling us about yourself, why you want to be part of this group, and why you would be a good member. You will need to decide soon, as membership will close shortly. After I receive an adequate letter, we will set up a time to talk face-to-face.

(Your First Name Only)

If you get another reply without the requested information, simply reply with the following sample.

Sample Reply – B2 (For a Second Insufficient Request)

(The Man's Name) You have not written a suitable correspondence as requested. All of the other prospective men have, so it would be unfair to them to consider you for membership. Therefore we are withdrawing you from consideration. I do hope that you find or create a group of men that you will be comfortable with.

(Your First Name Only)

You're done with him. No matter what he says, he would have been a drag on the group. Cut communications with him.

For the man asking about a nude group, a very simple, "Sorry, it is not the group for you."

Chapter 9:
The Face-to-Face

Seven Mistakes that Result in Failure

The final member selection is difficult, both emotionally and logistically. Some groups have attempted to take short cuts with group interviews, or tried to avoid the hard decision of telling a man that he isn't right for the group, or that he can't enter the group by an easier route. The following is a list of what not to do.

In many mythological stories, the hero finds warning signs that were left by the men who have walked the same path. These are my warning signs that I have left for you. Please heed them during this critical juncture.

1. *Don't Treat Men Like Animals*

   Some groups are organized by what I call the "Cattle Call" method, like a rush in the fraternities, where one simply advertises for anyone interested in forming a group of some kind to show up at a particular location at some set time. Once there, someone starts talking, maybe there is some mingling, or maybe it's like speed dating where you talk with everyone for a few minutes, ask them to fill out forms, and then tell them you will decide later if they made the cut. This is sometimes called the group interview. This is not a good idea. First, it sets up a hierarchy. The guy who does the talking is assumed to be the leader. If no one talks, and you just mingle, the reason for the choices will be unclear. Men who feel rejected will probably not want to try joining another group. It's thoughtless and juvenile and I don't know of any worthwhile men's groups that started this way. If there are, it isn't because of how they started; it is due to the tenacity of the men.

2. *Don't Use the Last Man Standing Approach*

Some groups have no entry procedures. Whoever shows up is in the group. You might also be tempted to allow anyone who is interested in joining to come. You might think, "I don't care if we have twenty guys. Those who are not really interested will drop out." Most likely the best men will be the first to recognize that the group is not functional and will leave.

Every time a man leaves the group, it's like a hole torn in the fabric. A strong group can survive, but a newly forming group often falls apart. You also have not raised the bar high enough to eliminate the men who are not committed to endure the process early on. Remember, you are designing an intentional community, not a haphazard swarm.

3. *Don't Meet with an Audience*

No spectators are allowed. Anyone who requests that they be permitted to come and observe a few meetings before deciding must be told that is not permitted. You must protect your group. The men in your group are not objects to be put on display. If a man is considering whether he wants to be a member of a men's group, he can read this book or do some research on the internet. Answer any questions that he has, provided that you do not break any confidences of the men that you have interviewed.

4. *Don't Let the Non-Committed In*

I mentioned earlier that the manual takes you through the first eight weeks. You will be asking each prospective member to commit to these eight meetings. Do not under any circumstances let anyone join who will not commit to the first eight meetings. If they cannot, or will not, they will never have the commitment needed to be a member.

5. *Don't Leave the Door Open*

Do not let any man join after the group has formed. Even if you have had men drop out of the group, do not permit new men to join for at least a year after the group has formed. If you do open the group up then, everyone must understand that the group will be formed anew with existing members and new members all being on equal ground.

6. *Don't Do a Sales Job*

Do not convince anyone to be part of your circle of men. That is backwards. A candidate should have the desire to connect and he should convince you to let him join you in this adventure.

7. *Don't Pity Men*

Never select a man because you pity him. If you find yourself thinking, "This guy really needs this group; we can help him," he is not a good candidate. The group is meant to be a circle of equals. It is unfair to select a man that you believe is unsuited for the challenge. The other reason not to select him is that he will likely fail, it will be your fault, and the group will be hurt.

Preparing for the Face-to-Face:

If you haven't already, make sure you have read through the entire book. You might want to make a list of questions to ask. Avoid questions like, "Where do you work?" "Where do you live?" Ask questions like, "What do you enjoy doing?" "What do you enjoy reading?" "What draws you to be interested in a men's group?" Keep the questions open-ended.

If you have not already decided when the group will meet, you will need to determine when the candidate is available for meetings at the face-to-face. One way of keeping track is to prepare a calendar ahead of time and to mark with an "X" any times that you cannot meet. If you have Indian Princesses with your daughter on Wednesday nights, that's out. If your spouse expects dinner and the movies on Saturday night, that's out. Then mark a "/" on times you would prefer not to meet. Now the mere preferences are a bit trickier. If you like *Iron Chef* on Sunday nights or can't miss Monday Night Football, those are priority decisions and are most likely a "/". However, if they are higher priorities than the group make an "X".

At each of the face-to-face meetings, compare your calendars. If another man cannot meet at a particular time "X" out the time. If he has a mere preference simply put a "/" on your calendar. If two men have an "X" a at the same time slot write "X-2", "X-3" etc. (Using pencil works best for this.) By the time you have met with every man you should have a time that works. If not, look at the calendar again and just decide. Sometimes it doesn't work out for everyone and sometimes men can change things if they must.

Remember, the group doesn't have to meet in the evening. Some groups meet before work, at long lunch breaks, or on the weekends. (Saturday mornings or Sunday nights work for some groups.) However, if you plan to meet at some time other than evenings, you should put it on the post. Most men will assume it is an evening event.

The face-to-face meeting should be set up in a public spot. Coffee shops are good, or have a soft drink at a fast food place. Having a beer might work, but alcohol can cloud your judgment, so I would avoid that setting. You can also meet for lunch, but be careful here, as not everyone can afford the same amount for lunch, or has the same amount of time. The meeting doesn't have to involve food or drink; you could meet at the mall, a library, or a park.

The General Conversation

It is natural to try to convince someone that what you're doing is good for them. Try to be a bit restrained and ask questions. It is as important for you to decide if he would make a good member as it is that he decides if this commitment is right for him.

If he has read the manual or visited the website, ask him what he thinks about the group's guidelines or the meeting formats or anything else. If you start to get stuck, use the questions you wrote out. Be sure that he understands that everyone in the group must share responsibility. Ask him about committing to the first eight meetings. If he is looking like a good candidate, then talk about what times are open for him. If you have decided he isn't right for the group, don't waste time with scheduling.

Evaluating a Candidate

As you are talking ask yourself these questions:

1. **Question:** Is he on time?

   Determination: This isn't a deal killer, but it's not good. Things do happen. If you have exchanged cell phone numbers, did he call? If other negative factors are present this could be the tipping point.

   If he is waiting for you and waves or approaches you when you walk in, he is the kind of outgoing guy you want.

2. **Question:** Has he read the manual or checked the website? Is he planning to get a copy of the book?

   Determination: If he has read the book, that's a good sign of a great member. He is taking ownership and understands what he is becoming involved with. If he has only checked the website, that's alright at this point.

   If he has no plans to get the manual, that might be a deal killer. For one man to refuse to expend the time and money that the other men have should not be acceptable. He will always feel he can be carried by the group. He is a parasite, not a group owner.

   If he is waiting for it from the library, that's ok.

   If he has it in hand and has filled it out, unless he is lacking in other ways, you've got yourself a member. (So, if you are the candidate, bring your manual; you already know what he will think.) Everyone in the group should always have access to the same information. A good men's group cannot be elitist. They function best when everyone knows what to expect. Access to information is the greatest leveler of social orders.

3. **Question:** Is he willing to help you? If he is one of the first to respond, ask him to put up some posters, or arrange for a room at the library. If he is one of the last, and he has read the book, consider asking him to run the first meeting or get name tags.

Determination: If he tells you that he doesn't want to or can't help, he will be a poor member. If he enthusiastically pitches right in, you've got a winner that will help carry the group.

4. **Question:** Does the conversation flow easily?

   Determination: A shared conversation is a good sign that he is listening and you are able to follow what he is saying. If he is delivering a monologue, be careful, particularly if that monologue stars him as the victim. If attempts to change the subject fail, you may not want this candidate.

5. **Question:** Is he <u>extremely</u> shy?

   Determination: It is sometimes hard to determine if a man is just reserved or extraordinarily shy. Does he look away when he speaks, or is he able to look you in the eye? Men who are extremely shy do not make very good members. They don't hold their ground in the group, they don't speak up, and they don't take ownership. They tend to drop out at the very first sign of conflict. Try asking him "What makes you excited?" Keep the questions very open, but if you are getting one word or short responses and no questions from him, you have to ask yourself, how much he will participate in the group?

6. **Question:** Is he outgoing, even a bit aggressive?

   Determination: Generally, you want outgoing and even somewhat aggressive men. You will always know where they stand and they will take ownership, and fight to keep the group together. But if from the conversation you think that their aggressiveness can or has crossed the line into violent behavior, reject them without hesitation. Conflict in a group is welcomed. Violence is not.

7. **Question:** Is he exhibiting any odd behaviors?

   Determination: If he seems manic (truly talking uncontrollably, not just a case of nervous chatter), disconnected (unable to follow the conversation), depressed (drifting off, or talking about suicide at your first meeting), or erratic (constantly changing topics), it's not going to work even if he has filled in the book. You are not a therapist. Some men may have mistaken your posting for some kind of free therapy group. It is not.

8. **Question:** Is he dogmatic in everything he says, or does he have an overwhelming political agenda?

   Determination: If he relentlessly raves against Muslims, rich white men, corporations, government, Democrats, Republicans, Jews, blacks, gays, Catholics, or any other group, beware. He is a dogmatist. He isn't going be open for discussion on a lot of issues. He will dominate the group with his endless diatribes, and if you get him under control, he will leave. Think about this carefully. Strongly-held views are acceptable and welcomed; endless dogmatic rants are not. Distinguishing between the two can be difficult.

   Also ask yourself if you are accepting his rants because you agree with him and like what he is saying, or if you are overly judgmental because you disagree with him and don't want your positions challenged. Probe a bit. Be fair but also be confident in your ability to decide. You will be able to figure out what you think the group should tolerate.

9. **Question:** Is he newly divorced?

   Determination: This is a difficult one. Sure it's fresh on his mind, and he may need support. If he seems stable in other ways, he could be a very good member. On the other hand, if he starts talking about having a restraining order against him, he might be too unstable for your group.

10. **Question:** Does he have a recent job loss?

    Determination: Ask him how he is handling it. He might be using it as an opportunity to change priorities, one of which is to have new friends. The loss of friends often accompanies the loss of a job today. This might have given him a new perspective. On the other hand, he might be so far on the edge that any honest observations made in the group could push him over.

11. **Question:** Has he recently suffered the death of a partner, child or parent?

    Determination: If this is a crisis-related group, of course, this might be a commonality. If not, how is he handling it? Has this precipitated a need for friends and can he handle the frankness of the group? Is he is showing signs of instability, or do you think his crisis would dominate the group or would hurt him? If not, he may prove to be a good member.

12. **Question:** Does everything he says define him as a victim?

    Determination: If so, then one day he will see himself as the victim of your group.

13. **Question:** Did you enjoy talking to him?

    Determination: Good sign, perhaps the best indication. Remember if you see him once a week for the next ten years, that's about 500 conversations. They will generally be as enjoyable or as tortured as the one you just completed.

Concluding the Face-to-Face:

By the end of the face-to-face, you should know whether he will be invited into the group. Tell him that, provided that he can commit to attending the first eight meetings, you would like to have him as a member.

If you know you don't want him in your group, say something like, "I don't think this group is for you. We really are more of a ...." or "I think that you really need more than this group can offer," or "I think you're really too brilliant for us, we are just ordinary guys trying to figure things out, but it was interesting learning about your collection of M16 Assault rifles and why God has told you whom to hate," or "You might want to start a group more specific to your needs." Remember he can start his own group. If he is not capable of starting a group suited to his needs, you don't want him anyway.

On the very rare occasion that you really can't decide, and you're not just trying to delay the inevitable, then say, "Give me a little time to think this over, you have really brought some things up that I need to reflect on. I will email you by…."

Chapter 10:
The First Eight Meetings

Meeting One – Adventure Time

Men will bond no matter what they are doing for eight weeks. If they, for example, went to ball games together for eight weeks, they would have some level of bonding. But if they do things that are more challenging, like boot camp, they will bond faster and closer. In addition, by following this manual, your group will acquire the communication tools that you will need for the group to function as a special kind of intentional community.

During these meetings there likely will be some conflict in the group. Because we are trying to be a community of men, we will not avoid it. We will welcome it and we will resolve it. After we do, we will be a more intimate group. If we avoid conflicts, our community will not develop.

Preparing for the Meeting

Contact everyone to let them know or to confirm the time and location of the meeting. Do this as soon as you know the details for sure. If you are emailing, I would suggest that you set up a group email on your contact list. Ask each man to reply back letting you know that they received the email. This is just a safety check. If someone doesn't reply, contact him. Email isn't as reliable as we think, and to leave a man hanging would not be good.

The initial organizer generally runs the first meeting. With the second meeting, leadership will change. The best way to do this is to put everyone else's name in an envelope or hat, and draw a name at each meeting. The man whose name is drawn will lead the next meeting.

A lot of men's groups have "talking sticks." When a man has the stick, he has the floor. No other man should interrupt him. Some say that the talking stick is a Native American tradition. I don't know if that's true, but I endorse the practice. The stick can be just a branch from trimming your hedge, or it can be an elaborate bundle of twigs that is highly decorated. If you don't have an artist in the group, here are a couple of suggestions. If you live in the city, you can simply get a large dowel rod 10 to 12 inches long from the lumber yard. Or, if you want a more symbolic stick, get a bundle of smaller rods. Tie them into a cylinder with a leather ribbon. I suggest sticking a little glue on them too, so they don't slide out. A story told by Aesop recounts how a dying father demonstrated to his sons that a single stick is easily broken, but a bundle of sticks is very strong. When men support one another they, too, are strong and can endure great forces. You can use anything, but it is nice to have some object that is a clear indication of who is speaking. Many groups do not use the talking stick throughout the meeting. Most use it at the meeting's opening and closing. But when conflict occurs, having one can help establish order. However, if you think a Talking Stick is silly, don't use one.

For the first meeting name tags are recommended. You might have met everyone, but they haven't met each other, and just hearing their name at the introductions isn't going to be enough for most men to remember them. Read through the agenda a few times thinking about how long each part will take. In the margin of the meeting agenda, write down the starting time, then plan the time needed for each item. For example, assuming a 7:30 start, if every man is given 3 minutes to speak near the beginning of the meeting, and you have 10 men, that is 30 minutes. If you plan to start this part of the meeting after 10 minutes of opening remarks at 7:40, that means that they will end at 8:10. This is just a guide in the margin. As long as you are within 10 minutes of your target, you're all right. Remember to plan a break about halfway through the meeting. The meeting should end on time.

Get to the meeting place at least 15 minutes ahead of time. If you have chosen your home as the meeting place, then be ready before everyone arrives. Have name tags and a large marker. If the men have your cell phone number, make sure your phone is on. If someone gets lost or delayed, they will be able to call. But once everyone has arrived, all phones should be off.

I have scripted in italics some portions of the first eight meetings with the exact words for you to say. Reading my words can be a comfort to the leader, and the group will know that they are following in the footsteps of a tried and true method. If you feel very comfortable in relating the same content in your own words, do so. You can do a combination of both, marking with a highlighter the parts you plan to read, and then just using your own words for the rest. If you read at the first meeting, the next guy will feel more comfortable doing so, too. But the final decision is always up to the meeting's leader.

Opening the Meeting

In your own words: Start by welcoming the men and telling them how pleased you are to see them, and thank everyone who helped you put up posters or did other work. Then if you have decided to have a "Talking Stick," introduce it as follows:

TALKING STICK

Say: *At times during the meeting, when it is important that only one man speaks, we will use this as our talking stick. When a man feels the need to have his say without interruption, he should ask for it. We will also use it during our opening round and our closing round.*

If you or another member has made a stick with special symbolism, explain it at this time. In some groups, a notch is made in the stick at the opening of each meeting. Over the years as the men look back over the many notches, they can visibly see a symbol of their journey together. If this is something you would like to do, do it now.

Choosing Next Week's Leader

Say: *We will follow the format of the* Men's Group Manual *for the first eight meetings. Then we will decide how we want to vary the meetings. The first order is to choose the leader for next week. I have put each of your names in this envelope.*

Ask someone to draw a name, and then announce the leader for the next meeting. Confirm that he will find a place to meet (if that has not already been arranged) and ask him to send a confirmation email to everyone. (You can draw names for all of the following meetings, or draw one name at each meeting.)

Opening Round

A round is a procedure where each man takes a turn speaking. The "Talking Stick" is typically passed to each man symbolizing that he is the only speaker. He should not be interrupted. When a meeting is started with a round it is called the Opening Round.

Say: *Next we will each say our name, how we learned about the group, how we are feeling right now, and one thing that we hope to obtain from the group. We have ___ men, so we need to keep these keep these comments to less than ___ minutes.*

Make your statement first, and then pass the stick to the next man. Complete the round and give a summary of the comments in your own words. It will be something like: *Most of us feel a bit nervous and excited about the meeting, as do I. Well, let's get started.*

First Exercise: Communication Awareness

Say: *In the first eight meetings we will acquire communication tools that will be useful in the group. While many of these will also be applicable to our lives outside of the group, they may not always be. Some of these exercises are uncomfortable at times. They are designed to be. Men who share difficult experiences bond more deeply.*

Because we are men involved in building something real that we care about, we will have conflict. Because we are creating an intentional community, we will welcome this conflict and using the communication tools that we will learn we will resolve it. Resolved conflict creates intimacy. This is one way in which this community will differ from another kind of organization. For example, in a business organization conflict is avoided. By avoiding conflict men become divided and controllable. Here, we are free men. Here we will build a community in which we will be our authentic selves without fear of consequences.

In our working-life and in polite society, we have learned many dances that permit us to avoid ownership of our statements, our feelings, and even our lives. In this group, we are going to learn to break these taboos. We will start slowly at first, and by the end of the eight weeks we will have learned new skills that will be used to communicate between ourselves as authentic men.

One of these dances tends to always be performed when men meet. I call it the Question and Answer dance. In this dance we wait to be asked a question before we speak. This narrows the conversation and typically starts with, "What do you do?" "Where do you live?" etc. This generally avoids any possibility of a meaningful conversation. Another aspect of the dance that some men engage in is to never own their statements. They start comments with, "they say," "some people," "you," etc. Here, there is no need to control or to be afraid of what we say. Here, we will own our words.

Say: *Select another man. Someone you don't know will be best. Begin talking, but* **do not ask any questions**. *Talk about anything you like, except your profession. In the group you are not defined by your profession, and while it is not taboo to talk about, it is not your identity in the group. Speak freely in a back and forth exchange. OK, let's start.* (If there is an uneven number of men, form one group of three.)

The leader must also participate in all the exercises.

In five minutes stop the men.

Ask: *How did that feel?*

If a period of silence follows, let it be. You don't have to call on men or give them permission to talk. Wait until at least some have spoken. If everyone has not spoken, ask if anyone else wants to say anything. If no one replies, move on.

Second Exercise: Ownership of Your Statements

Say: *We are going to do this a little longer; this time, however,* **EVERY** *statement you make* **MUST** *start with* **"I."** *Starting with "I" is the first step in taking ownership of your statements. Later you will each introduce your partner and tell the group something about him.*

In six or seven minutes stop the men again.

Ask: *Tell us how you felt, by making an "I" statement. If any man does not start his comment with an "I," it is the responsibility of every man to help him.*

Talk about how it felt for a few minutes or until the energy ends.

Say: *"I" statements are very important not only for owning our thoughts and feelings but also for solving conflicts. There is a difference between, "You are a jerk for interrupting me," and "I feel devalued when I am interrupted." The first statement is a judgment and assumes knowledge that you don't have; the second is ownership of information that only you have and need to share in order for your feelings to be known. We will work with this concept more over the next meetings.*

If anyone has comments, take a few minutes, otherwise move on.

Say: *Now, let's go around the room. I want each man to introduce the man he partnered with and I want to hear something that you learned about him. I will start.*

Proceed around the room. Then call everyone back together.

Third Exercise: Introducing the Laws and Guidelines

This next task can go very quickly or it can be very difficult. Take all the time you need. If you don't finish, then continue next week. If agreement cannot be reached on the meaning of these three basic laws by the end of the second meeting (although I have never heard of this happening) divide the group into two different men's groups, get more members, and start over. These laws are vitally important to the success of the group.

The Laws

Law One: Take Responsibility

Law Two: Tell the Truth as You Believe It

Law Three: Maintain Confidentiality

Say: *The Laws: These are absolutes that can never be changed. Take out your manuals. Each man must read them, and then we must agree on what they mean. After every man is clear on their meaning, and is in agreement with their meaning he will sign his book. A man placing his name on a page symbolizes his honor. It is a visible meaningful act. (Name) will you read the first law and the discussion topics.*

Then ask other men to read the other two.

Law One: Take Responsibility

You are responsible to the group. You are accountable for getting what you want from the group, for letting the group know when you feel that you have been heard, and when you have not been heard. You are responsible for telling the group what is important to you, for building group trust, for nurturing and supporting the group. You are not just an attendee; you are an owner/operator of the group. You are responsible to accept leadership and to support the leader. When you are the leader, you are responsible to maintain the order of the group. This means that sometimes you will be confronted with conflicts that you will work to resolve rather than to avoid.

Taking responsibility also means being in the present, keeping your focus at the meetings and participating. Participating means helping the other men understand their story. At times, it might mean pointing out contradictions, or asking them how they feel, or giving feedback.

(Call for Discussion)

Law Two: Tell the Truth as You Believe It

This is a hard one because we often don't know what the truth is. Our truth changes from week to week. You might be an avid atheist one week, and then a week later a born-again Christian. The law does not require that you be right, or that you can never change, but it demands that you are true to who you are. Don't pretend to be something else. This doesn't mean that you have to share every detail of your life. It only means that when you do share aspects of your life, you are truthful. For example, a man might be talking about a drug issue he is having, and another man in the group might have had a long history with drug rehab, or also currently be struggling. Even so, he is not required to share that. Not sharing is not dishonest. But if he were to say, "I've never had an issue with drugs," then he is not telling the truth. While this example is about a factual issue, men are much more likely to be dishonest about their feelings. Tell the truth; if you can't tell the truth, then pass and say nothing.

Any man can pass, without a reason if he doesn't want to say or participate in something. The group can't force him or ask him why. The group has a responsibility to support him and to assume nothing by his pass.

(Call for Discussion)

Law Three: Maintain Confidentiality

What is said in the group stays in the group. This may seem simple but are there exceptions? Discuss each of the examples below and go around the group getting everyone's input. There may be disagreement, and that's all right. You might not decide on everything tonight. It is important to make this issue personal. Every man has to have a clear understanding of what he may tell his partner or others outside the group who ask about his men's group. These are hard questions.

What is confidential?

In discussing this issue sometimes men have different delineations of confidentiality. Some men believe that anything can be shared with anyone outside the group provided that they first say that it is confidential. This is a bit like telling a reporter that it is "off the record." Others maintain absolute adherence and will not reveal anything, even to save a life. Most men are somewhere in between. Wherever your group ends up is correct for you. But be clear.

An example

If a man admits that he is abusing a child, his wife, or is planning to commit or has committed a murder, is it permissible in order to protect innocent people to break confidentiality? Professions with confidentiality rules deal with these issues. If a man tells a teacher that he is abusing a child, she must report it. Attorneys must not. A priest might be obligated to report a confidence learned in a teaching situation, but if told in the confessional, he must not.

If a man does report a group member to an authority, is he responsible to tell that man that he was the one who turned him in?

(Call for Discussion)

If a man talks about less serious crimes, like embezzlement, using illegal drugs, or soliciting prostitutes, is it permissible to break confidentiality? Again, if a man does report someone to an authority, is he responsible to inform the man that he did it?

(Call for Discussion)

If a man doesn't use the other member's name, is it permissible to discuss information with someone outside the group? The "I know a guy who" type of story? Is he crossing the line here? While he is not directly revealing the person's identity, he is revealing his story. Is the story his to tell? If he explicitly asks the man if he can share this story, then can he tell it even if he learned it in the group?

(Call for Discussion)

Is it permissible to tell someone within the group what was revealed by another man during a meeting that he missed? Your group has to decide and be clear about it.

(Call for Discussion)

Who is in the circle of confidentiality?

Is it only the men in the group? What about the men's partners?

(Call for Discussion)

What is <u>not</u> confidential?

It is as important to be clear about what a man can say as it is to be clear about what he can't say. By discussing and agreeing to both, clear lines are defined.

An example

Is it permissible to say, "We did several interesting exercises to develop communication skills?" Basically, that reveals nothing more than what anyone can get from the website or the manual. That is probably not confidential because the information is in the open market.

(Call for Discussion)

Is it permissible to say, "There are ten men in our group? Clyde is in his fifties, is married, has three children and is an architect. Tom is a..." Basically this is what I call "directory information," the kind of information anyone could find in any number of listings with your name. Groups typically permit this kind of information to be revealed, but some do not.

(Call for Discussion)

Is it permissible to say, "I brought up my issues of... and I was given very helpful advice..." If a man is sharing his own issues, he certainly can talk about them with others, but can he say that he told the group? What about talking about the advice he got in the group outside of the group? Where is the line?

(Call for Discussion)

After the Laws and what they mean are agreed to, then the Guideline discussion starts.

Guidelines

The guidelines are designed to help the group run better.

Say: *Now we will discuss our guidelines. Guidelines are merely procedures to help the group run better. They can be changed with the group consensus. We can change them now or as needed over the evolution of our group. I will read the proposed guidelines one at a time and ask for discussion. If there is no discussion I will ask if everyone agrees, then we will go around the circle and one at a time each man will say "agree" or "disagree." If there is a single disagreement discussion will continue. If there is discussion, then I will attempt to write down and read what I believe the group is agreeing to. Then in like manner we will go around the circle again saying "agree" or "disagree." We will continue until every man is in agreement. We might also agree to reject any of these guidelines for any reason we want. Remember Law One, you have agreed to be responsible for making your desires known. This is the first test of Law One.*

Guideline One: Late or Absent

If you are going to be late or absent, call or email someone.

(Call for Discussion)

Guideline Two: Meeting Confirmation

The group leader is responsible to send out an email or call each member confirming the meeting location.

(Call for Discussion)

Guideline Three: Smoking

No smoking during the meeting. (Some groups permit smoking, or take breaks; decide what you want)

(Call for Discussion)

Guideline Four: Alcohol/Drugs

No one is to be impaired by alcohol or other drugs during the meeting. (Some groups have specific guidelines like no use within 24 hours of the meeting; some groups do permit drinking if it is an event meeting like a dinner or ball game, etc.)

(Call for Discussion)

Guideline Five: Cellphones

No cellphone use during the meeting, unless permission is asked at the beginning of the meeting. (Permission might be asked to leave a cell phone on because of a potential emergency, professional call or a member has not been heard from, etc. Some groups permit cell phone use during breaks.)

(Call for Discussion)

Guideline Six: Leaving the Group

Should a man decide to leave the group, because he no longer can be or he no longer wants to be a member, he will attend an exit meeting. (See Chapter 14) This might seem like an odd topic to be talking about at your first meeting, but it will happen that men will move away, have dramatic changes in their lives, or simply decide that they no longer want to be committed to the group. When this happens it is important that there is a way to leave that does the least harm to the group. Now is the time to discuss and make that commitment.

(Call for Discussion)

As other issues arise, guidelines can be added or modified by agreement.

Our group has added the following guideline:

_____

_____

_____

_____

_____

Say: *Read the next paragraph in you manuals as I read it aloud. Then sign it as your word that you are in agreement with the statement.*

I have noted any changes in the laws and guidelines that the group has made, I have made all of my objections clear, and we have reached an agreement that I understand and that I can support. I agree that these are the laws and guidelines of the group.

Sign _____.

If time permits, you can do a Question Round. This is simple. The leader asks a question and every man replies. Suitable questions for tonight might be:

"What is the most important benefit you hope the group will provide?"

"What was the most difficult part of deciding to join the group?"

"Did you hesitate before coming tonight?"

"If you have family, are they supportive of your involvement in this group?"

You might think of other questions. If you are near the end of your time, close the meeting. If you didn't get through all the laws and guidelines, then they will be covered at the next meeting. Leave ten to fifteen minutes at the end of the meeting for a Closing Round.

Closing Round

As the group opened with the ritual of the Opening Round, the group will end with a shorter whip round. A Whip Round is any round that is less than one minute per man.

Say: *We have reached the end of our first meeting. We will end this meeting with a Closing Round. I want each man to say how he is feeling now, and to tell the group if he will be honoring his commitment by returning next week.*

The reason I have added the confirmation to return is that even though every man has made a commitment, it is reassuring for him to hear that the other men will also honor their commitments. There may be moments during the next week when the men question returning. This intentional community is a culture shock that affects each man differently. For some, it's exciting, for others terrifying, for others it may not seem that much different from their normal way of behaving. The more each man shares his commitment, the easier it will be for everyone.

If the group has a Talking Stick, give it and any other items, such as nametags, the envelope of names, and other supplies to next week's leader. He is now responsible.

Congratulations! You have completed your first meeting.

My Notes

Every man should keep personal notes regarding his meeting.

What are my feelings about this meeting, what do I want to remember, and what did I learn?

_____

_____

_____

_____

Meeting Two – Awareness

Sometime during the week following the first meeting, some men may have a feeling that they don't want to go back. This bit of discomfort is normal, particularly if this experience is new. A second feeling some men may have is the "I shouldn't have said that," or "I should have said this." Anything you said was the right thing to say at the moment or you wouldn't have said it. If any man rejects you or the group because of what was said, he never understood what the group was about and wasn't really committed to the community. If you want to clarify something you said, or add to it, do it during the Opening Round at the next meeting.

The second meeting in many ways is even more important than the first. Who will return is an overwhelming concern. If everyone does return, congratulations to the group are in order. If someone drops out, it is better now than after the group has bonded. A departure hurts the group; recognize that fact at the beginning of the meeting. Let it sink in and then move on. It is a bit like a death in a community. It is very important that no one accepts the blame for the person leaving. No one need think, "I must have caused him to leave because I said…" He decided to end his adventure. He may not have been ready, he might have misunderstood the purpose the group, or there may be reasons we can never know. However, no one in the group caused him to end his commitment.

This meeting will again focus on communication skills and will begin to bring together some of the structure, or rituals, that the meetings will include.

Like each of the first eight meetings, I will script the meeting for you, but if you feel more comfortable using your own words, feel free to do so.

Preparing for the Meeting

Contact everyone to remind them of the meeting time and location, and provide a map if needed. I think it is a good procedure that everyone replies to the email with a few words that acknowledge the receipt of the email. The leader should always be ready at least fifteen minutes ahead of time. Make sure you have the envelope with the remaining names in it if you haven't already assigned a leader for all the meetings.

Have a list with everyone's first and last name on it and two columns, one for email and one for phone numbers. Ask the men to write down the information they want you to provide to the other group members. Some men may be more cautious than others. Some may have more than one email; let everyone write down what they want to share. It will be your responsibility as this week's leader to type it up and email it out, or print copies and bring them to the next meeting for men who do not have email.

Remember to plan a break about halfway through the meeting. Some groups have a snack and beverage during break. If refreshments are served, they can be provided by that week's leader or your group could have another man assigned each week to the task.

Name tags are not needed for this meeting. Instead we will be playing a game to help learn everyone's name.

Opening the Meeting

If you have decided to have a "Talking Stick," hold it at the opening. In your own words: start by welcoming the men and telling them how pleased you are to see them again and introduce the topic of the meeting. If anyone is missing, acknowledge the fact and tell the men that, right after the Opening Round, you will do a second round for everyone to express any feelings they may have regarding the missing man.

Opening Round

Keep the Opening Round short. If any man starts to delve into an issue, tell him that rounds are for a short check in and that you will reserve some time later in the meeting for him to raise his issue. Ask him how much time he may need and then reserve time later in the meeting for him. It's important not to forget to give him the time. But right now don't let him derail the meeting. It is extremely important because a new group needs structure in order to give less aggressive men room to express themselves.

Say: *We are at our second meeting; we will begin with an Opening Round. Remember the Opening Round is a time to check in. A time for each man to take 3 to 4 minutes to tell the group what is happening in his life since the last meeting and how he is feeling right now. Another element of a round that can be included, if the leader wants to, is called "The Query." The Query is a question that might introduce the theme of the meeting, start a topic, or just be fun. Remember, any man can pass on the Query if he wants to. Tonight I'm including a Query, "Name one thing you like about yourself." I would like the man at my right to start.*

If you want to substitute another question for the Query, feel free to do so. These Queries can be useful in bringing up topics related to the meeting, raising an uncomfortable issue, and for getting to know everyone.

If a man has left the group, the leader should now ask each man to express how they are feeling about it with another round, again passing the stick. Disappointment, anger, and hurt are all typical feelings; the leader sums up the group's expressions.

Choosing Next Week's Leader

Ask someone to draw a name from the envelope, and then announce the leader for the next meeting. Confirm that he will find a place to meet (if that has not already been arranged) and ask him to send a confirmation email to everyone.

First Exercise: The Name Game

Say: *We are going to play the Name Game. This is how it works. Say your first name then say something you like that starts with the same letter as your first name. It must start with the same letter and be a noun, something that can be easily visualized. For example, "My name is Clyde and I like clowns." Or "My name is Henry and I like hens." Then the second man says: "He is Clyde and he likes clowns. My name is Bill and I like bikes." The third man recites the first two, and then adds his own name and like. By the time it gets back to the first man everyone is included. Now the fun starts. Keep going one more round so that every man says every man's name and what he likes. By the time you have done this everyone should know everyone's name, but if you forget, just ask. Remember, the rules of social order, where it might be rude to ask for a name again after having been introduced once, don't apply here.*

Second Exercise: Awareness

Say: *Becoming aware of awareness might sound redundant but it's not. In all existence there are only two elements. One is the "I" and the other is "The Other." The Other is a way of naming everything else that is not "I". Each man is aware of his body parts, but he is not those parts. If he loses a leg, the "I" is not diminished. Even if he should suffer brain damage, the "I" is still present undiminished. Therefore, for this exercise, I have included in the awareness of everything other than the "I," our bodies, our emotions, our thoughts, others around us, our environment and all the externalities that we experience. We can improve our awareness of this "other" by understanding and monitoring our awareness and finely honing this skill. Like an athlete works his body to build strength, we will sharpen our minds to improved awareness.*

Last week we worked on the awareness of "I" and how important using "I" statements are for owning our thoughts and our emotions. Tonight we are beginning awareness of everything else. The more aware we become of our self, the more we understand both our strength and our weakness. To help us become more aware, the other men will help us. Remember the words of the poet Robert Burns,

> *"O would some Power the gift to give us,*
> *To see ourselves as others see us!*
> *It would from many a blunder free us."*

At times, honest feedback can be painful. But always remember: the worse the truth, the better the friend that tells you. Here, we are building trust. Trust is not built on the "little white lies" of refined culture. Trust is built on truth-telling. Remember the Laws of the group. Tell the truth as we see it.

Read or ask another man to read the four ways that we experience awareness:

Awareness occurs in four forms; they are:

1. **Sensation.** We experience our surroundings through our physical senses - sight, smell, taste, touch, and hearing. While visual observation and hearing are most often used, we will utilize the word sensation because it is more inclusive. Sensation can only make us aware of our physical experience.

2. **Intuitive Intelligence.** We have insight, an inner perception, a moral compass, and an understanding of consistency that we bring to our awareness. We may see something and know that it is good, or that there is danger. I believe this intuitive ability is in our genetic code. We are born with it for survival. Many top security experts teach that trusting these instincts can save your life.

3. **Intellect.** We are thinking beings. As René Descartes said, "Cogito, ergo sum." ("I think, therefore I am.") Thinking is the process of interpreting our awareness based on our experience. Sometimes this can create a false awareness. We might interpret someone telling us that our socks don't match as an attempt to injure us by insulting our ability to dress properly, when in fact the man was attempting to be of assistance to us by making us aware.

4. **Emotion.** These are our body's responses to events. They are our feelings - sad, mad, glad, scared. Again, using the above matching socks example, I would react with anger if I concluded that I was being insulted. Conversely, I would react with gratitude if I felt that I was being helped.

   Be alert to how these four elements of awareness interact as we increase our consciousness.

Call for discussion. Let this run up to ten minutes.

Part One

Say: *Choose a partner, someone you have not worked with yet. If there is an odd number, I will join one of the groups. Move your chairs so that you are sitting directly facing your partner. First, we will be aware of our ability to be aware by using our senses. As you are looking at your partner say what you see. (For example, "I am aware of your grey*

T-shirt. I am aware of your blue eyes.) For this exercise, we are only being aware of objective data. Do not use words like "sad eyes" or "interesting shirt." Take turns talking.

After about 4 or 5 minutes, call a break, and ask for discussion.

Say: *What was your experience like? Did you feel limited?*

Say: *We are going to continue and now try to look at the more subtle body language, but again offer no interpretations. For example, say, "I am aware that your arms are folded," or "I am aware that you are leaning forward, "but do not say, "You seem defensive," or "Your posture is aggressive." Again, alternate.*

Stop the group after two to three minutes and ask for discussion.

Part Two

Say: *Now we are going to include intuitive knowledge. Without thinking about why, just tell your partner what you are sensing about him. For example: "I sense you are extremely uncomfortable, "or "I sense you are bored." Again alternate.*

In two minutes, again call for discussion.

Remember to take a break at some time.

Part Three

Say: *Now we are going to move to intellect. That is interpreting what we see based on our experiences. Say what you are aware of through your senses or intuition and then how you interpret it. Each statement should start with the awareness and then the interpretation. Also, I hope everyone is remembering to use the "I" statement. For example "I see your T-shirt and think you are a casual kind of guy. I sense you are uncomfortable and think you are a shy man." "I see you sitting straight, looking directly at me, and I think you are a confident man."*

After 3 or 4 minutes, stop the group but without discussion.

Say: *Now just sit there, looking directly at one another without any thought or interpretation. Just sit face to face.*

After one minute, ask for discussion. Say: *How was interpretation (thinking) different from just sitting? Which type of awareness, interpretation or non-interpretation, do we generally use in the day-to-day world? Why?*

Part Four

Say: *Now we are going to switch focus. This time, be aware of your body and how you interpret your awareness. For example; "I am aware that my body is sweating and I think it's because I'm stressed." or "I am aware that my body is slouching. I think it is because it is tired."*

After about three minutes stop the group and again just sit, being aware of oneself for a minute and then start a discussion.

Part Five

Say: *Just talk together about the exercise and clear up any misconceptions that your partner may have had. Otherwise, just chat. But as you do, try to be aware of how you are understanding your partner through the three kinds of awareness that we worked on tonight: Sensation, Intuitive Intelligence, and Intellect. Next week, we will spend most of the meeting on the fourth kind of awareness –Emotion.*

Third Exercise: Reflection

Point out that there is space at the end of each chapter in the manual to take notes. These notes should contain the men's reflections on their experience, but they should never include anything that is confidential.

In your notes for this meeting, also write down your goals for the men's group. What do you want to get from this experience? If you want to take time from the meeting to do this you may, otherwise it is a good homework assignment. These notes will be needed for the eighth meeting.

Depending on the time left, the leader needs to decide how to use the remainder of the time. Here are the priorities.

1. If someone brought up an issue in the Opening Round that they want time to discuss, do that now.

2. If the group has formed around specific issues or needs, for example if the group was started to deal with issues facing divorced fathers, then the leader might begin the discussion by asking every man to mention the most pressing issue facing him.

3. If the group was a more general group, then you might want to do some "Get to Know Everyone Better Rounds." These can be simple, things like "Do you have children, how many?" Another way of getting to know everyone is having every man write a question on a card, shuffle them, and then read the question and ask everyone to respond to it. During these discussions, practice what you have learned. First, own your words, by using "I" statements. Second, be aware of how you are aware and how the other men are expressing their awareness.

4. You might want to do another round of the Name Game to make sure the names have stayed with everyone.

Closing the Meeting

About 15 minutes before the end of the meeting, start the Closing Round.

Say: *We are now going to do our Closing Round. This is a round telling the group how you are feeling and any unfinished business. Unfinished business can be anything from wanting to say thank you to the leader to saying that you felt hurt when you were cut off by another man while you were talking. Don't leave without saying what you need to say, or it will be with you all week.*

Give the stick and any other group materials to the next leader and if you have adopted a closing ritual, do it.

Remember to type up the contact information and send it out to everyone.

Congratulations on completing your second meeting!

My Notes

Every man needs to respond to the following questions before the next meeting.

What do I want from the group in the next six weeks?

_____

_____

_____

_____

_____

_____

_____

What do I want from the group in the next year?

_____

_____

_____

_____

_____

_____

_____

_____

What should I remember when it's my turn to lead the meeting?

_____

_____

_____

_____

_____

_____

_____

What was my experience like in this meeting?

_____

_____

_____

_____

_____

Meeting Three – I Feel that I Feel

The last meeting covered three aspects of awareness but did not cover one of the most important aspects of awareness: Emotions.

Emotions for men are sometimes difficult, and we are generally not very well trained in recognizing them. We are taught that thinking is more worthwhile than emotions, so sometimes we try to define our emotions as reasons. In this meeting, we will complete several exercises to contrast thinking with feeling.

Preparing for the Meeting

Contact everyone reminding them of the location and provide a map if needed. By now everyone should be in the habit of responding to the group leader reassuring him that they got the information. The leader should always be ready at least fifteen minutes ahead of time. Make sure you have the envelope with the remaining names in it.

Decide if nametags are needed or if the Name Game was sufficient for learning everyone's name.

Remember to plan a break about halfway through the meeting. Some groups have a snack and beverage during the break. The refreshments are generally provided by that week's leader. This is not necessary and can vary from meeting to meeting as the leader wishes.

Opening the Meeting

Welcome everyone to the meeting and introduce the meeting's topic. If a man has left the group the leader should mention it and plan a separate round to talk about it before moving on.

The leader for any part of the meeting always has the option of asking another man to read any portion of an exercise. If a particular meeting has a lot of presentations this may help to hold interest and take some of the pressure off the group leader.

Opening Round

Keep the Opening Round short. I have suggested a Query related to tonight's meeting. If you would rather make one up, you certainly can.

Say: *We are at our third meeting; we will begin with our Opening Round. Remember the Opening Round is a time to check in. A time for each man to take 2 to 3 minutes to tell the group what is happening in his life since the last meeting and how he is feeling right now. The Query for this meeting is "What emotion do you feel most often?"*

Second Round

Do a fast round of the Name Game. Help anyone who can't remember. This should implant all the names. Try to call the men by their names throughout the meeting.

Choosing Next Week's Leader

Ask someone to draw a name from the envelope, and then announce the leader for the next meeting. Confirm that he will find a place to meet (if that has not already been arranged) and ask him to send a confirmation email to everyone.

First Exercise: Thinking and Feeling

Say: *Last week we practiced three of the four ways that awareness occurs. For review, the four ways are:*

1. **Sensation.** We experience our surroundings through our physical senses - sight, smell, taste, touch and hearing.

2. **Intuitive Intelligence.** We have insight, an inner perception, a moral compass, and an understanding of consistency that we bring to our awareness.

3. **Intellect.** Thinking is interpreting our awareness based on our experience.

4. **Emotion.** These are our body's responses to events: sad, mad, glad, and scared.

As we become more self-aware, we will notice also that we begin to understand the complexity of our feelings. Often there are other feelings hiding behind our emotions. For example, a man might become very angry at a stop light when the car ahead of him doesn't hit the gas the moment the light changes. But he might in fact be really angry about his job, and therefore waited until the last moment to leave for work. He is transferring his anger to the other driver, whom he can now blame for his impending tardiness.

In this meeting, we are going to work on expressing our emotions and understanding the contrast between feeling and thinking.

Emotional Feelings *are body responses that might be triggered by sensation, intuition, or thinking. They occur within us; therefore it is an internal awareness rather than an external awareness. Are they created by us or do they arise within us? The emotional reactions of different men to identical data might be diametrically opposed, even when they interpret the data the same and have the same intuitive understanding. By being aware of our emotions and what the triggers are behind them, can we control them? Or, do they always control us? If we can control our emotions, what would be the advantage and what would be the disadvantage? Is simply understanding them, in order to make clearer decisions, a more reasonable goal than control?*

(Open discussion until the energy wanes.)

Say: *Examples of awareness that trigger emotions are: A sensation of intense heat might trigger fear, an intuitive knowing that we are loved might trigger happiness, or a calculation that the amount of remaining food will result in our children being hungry might trigger fear and sadness.*

Four Categories of Emotions

1. **Happy**: glad, delighted, joyful, cheerful, blissful, pleased, in high spirits, warm, excited

2. **Sad:** depressed, gloomy, miserable, cheerless, heartbroken, distressed, discouraged, worried, dismayed, upset, mournful, sorrowful, somber, doleful

3. **Angry:** mad, annoyed, irritated, fuming, livid, heated, incensed, frustrated, teed off, enraged, seething, furious, irate

4. **Scared:** frightened, afraid, terrified, fearful, petrified, nervous, worried, anxious, uneasy, fretful, apprehensive, troubled, disturbed, perturbed, tense

While there are many more words to describe and nuance these emotions, using these four simplified categories will help us to identify our awareness.

Say: *We will now do a Thinking Round: Let's go around fast, each man making a thinking statement. For example: "I think this room is uncomfortably hot." He is interpreting his awareness of the temperature. Or "I think the Cincinnati Reds will win the World Series." Again, he is interpreting his awareness of the data. Remember, a thinking statement doesn't have to be correct. He may well be misinterpreting the data, based on experience or, in the case of the Reds winning the World Series, false hopes. But he is still interpreting information. When thinking, we can always be wrong. We can also question someone's thinking and discover where and why we draw different conclusions. Let's begin.*

Go around twice.

Say: *Now we are going to do a feeling round. For example, "I feel terrific right now." or "I am worried about my job." These are internal feelings; they cannot be questioned by anyone because only the person feeling the emotion can know what he feels. It is not based on objective data or a method of interpretation.*

If the man who said, "I am worried about my job" had said, "We lost a major client so I think my job is in jeopardy," that would not have been an emotion. That would have been a thinking calculation. Everyone has an obligation to correct any misstatements.

Again, two fast rounds.

Second Exercise: Awareness of Deep Personal Emotions

You may not be able to finish this exercise. Don't rush it. If you only do one round, it's a good meeting. I suggest for these kinds of rounds that the talking stick be used in order to clearly signal who has the floor. These might be more intense rounds than in the past, and may bring up some deep issues. If so, take a breath, this is a safe place. Don't be afraid to demonstrate support. Don't move on before everyone is ready.

Part One: Scared

Say: *Now look at the list of words related to the word "Scared." Take a minute and then we will do a slower round where each man tells one thing that is making him scared (nervous, worried, anxious, troubled, disturbed). Use the word and then give an explanation. This is one of the first times that each man is beginning to reveal his emotional self to the others. For example, "I'm worried because my son is falling behind in school," or "I'm terrified that I might have cancer," or "I'm anxious that the men in the group won't like me when they learn that I'm an ex-priest."*

Even though just one sentence and one reason for fear was used in the examples, take all the time you need to explain the full story of what's going on in your life. What are you finding fearful? If we don't finish tonight, we can return to this at some future meeting. It is not important that we get through every emotion. What is important is that we learn to be aware of our feelings and that we share them, so that we may truly understand, trust, and know each other.

Part Two: Angry

Say: *Now look at the list of words related to the word "angry." We will do a round where each man tells one thing that is making him angry (mad, annoyed, irritated, fuming, livid, heated, incensed, teed off, enraged, seething, furious, irate). As before, use the word and then give the reason. For example, "I'm angry because I believe my son doesn't appreciate what I do for him." "I'm enraged because I believe I might have cancer." "I'm teed off because I feel devalued when some of the men in the group come late." Notice I used one of the same reasons before in the "scared" example. Men can have different or multiple emotions related to the same stimulus. As the group develops, it will be increasingly important to be aware of all the emotions surrounding an issue. Again, this can be an intense round. Don't limit yourself to one sentence or cause. Take all the time you need to communicate your feelings.*

Part Three: Sad

Say: *Now look at the list of words related to the word sad. Take a minute and we will do a round where each man tells one thing that has, or is making him sad (depressed, gloomy, miserable, cheerless, heartbroken, distressed, discouraged, worried, dismayed, upset, mournful, sorrowful, somber, doleful). Use the word and then give the reason. For example, "I'm heartbroken because my best friend moved away," or "I'm sad that I might have cancer."*

Take the time you need.

Part Four: Happy

Say: *Now look at the list of words related to the word happy. Take a minute and then we will do a happy round where each man tells one thing that is making him happy (glad, delighted, joyful, cheerful, blissful, pleased, in high spirits, warm, excited). Use the word and then give the reason. For example, "I'm delighted that I found this group," or "I'm pleased that there are so many treatments for cancer."*

Closing the Meeting

About 15 minutes before the end time of the meeting, in your own words, start the Closing Round. Again you most likely did not complete all the emotion rounds, but the men are beginning to share their emotions and trust is building.

Give the stick and any other group materials to the next leader. If you have adapted a closing ritual, do it.

Congratulations you have made it through the third meeting!

My Notes

Every man should keep personal notes regarding his meeting.

What did I learn about myself?

_____

_____

_____

_____

_____

_____

What should I remember when it's my turn to lead the meeting?

_____

_____

_____

_____

_____

_____

_____

Meeting Four– I Hear You

Preparing for the Meeting:

Make sure you have a meeting place, the envelope, and the talking stick, and that you have sent out an email and read the meeting script.

Opening the Meeting

Welcome everyone to the meeting and introduce the meeting's topic, listening. Listening is a super skill to have. Most of the time people fail to listen, either because a man thinks he is too important to listen to someone else, or he is too worried about what he is going to say so he is rehearsing in his mind while the other guy is talking, or simply because he has never learned to listen. Remember, listening has little to do with hearing, and more to do with understanding and being interested in the other person. It has been said that in a relationship, it is better to be interested than interesting. This meeting will work on building listening skills.

The leader always has the option of asking another man to read any portion of an exercise. If a particular meeting has a lot of presentations, this will often help hold interest and take some of the pressure off the group leader.

Opening Round

Keep the Opening Round short. I have suggested a Query related to tonight's meeting. If you would rather make one up, you certainly can.

Say: *We are at our fourth meeting; we will begin with an Opening Round. The Query for this meeting is "In a word or phrase, what describes good listening?"*

After the Opening Round the leader should sum up the feelings of the group.

Choosing Next Week's Leader

Ask someone to draw a name from the envelope, and then announce the leader for the next meeting. Confirm that he will find a place to meet (if that has not already been arranged) and ask him to send a confirmation email to everyone.

First Exercise: Four Ways of Conversation

Say: *At this meeting we are going to experience four different ways men talk to each other. You might have experienced some of them already. But we are going to dramatize them in order to recognize them more easily. Pick a man in the group with whom you haven't worked before. Arrange your chairs to be facing one another. After I give the instructions, one of you will play the role of the first man and the other the second. When I say switch, you will reverse the roles.*

Wait until everyone is situated. If there is an odd number, join one of the groups making it three.

Part 1: Ignored

Say: *First man using the name of the second man will ask him to tell something interesting about himself. For example, "Bob, tell me something interesting about yourself."*

But when the second man, Bob in our example, talks, the first man ignores him, looks away, checks his phone, fidgets with his book or rolls his eyes, does anything except pay attention. I want the second man to keep talking no matter how he feels until I say stop. Ready, start.

After about two minutes,

Say: *Stop and switch roles asking the same question again.*

After two more minutes,

Say: *Stop.*

Say: *How did that feel? Have you ever experienced that feeling before?*

What was your emotional response? Did you feel listened to? How did you interpret the listener's actions?

Continue discussion only as long as needed.

Part 2: The Thief

Say: *Start with the same question: For example "Bob, tell me something interesting about yourself." But this time after a few words the first guy cuts in picking up on a few key words. For example, if Bob starts talking about meeting Robert Bly, the first guy might say, "Well when I read* Iron John, *I understood the story completely even before he explained it." Only let the second guy back in long enough to steal the conversation again and again.*

Give this about two minutes and then,

Say: *Switch.*

After another two minutes again ask the group for discussion, ask them how they felt.

Part 3: Connected Listening

Say: *We will again ask the same question but this time we will make eye contact, and respond appropriately. No cut-offs or stealing the conversation. Rather than me saying switch, you must invite a transition from one speaker to the next. Typically, this is done by asking a question at the end of your statement(s).*

For example, first man says, "Bob tell me something interesting about yourself."

Bob replies, "I like to grow heirloom tomatoes."

First man asks, "What is your favorite kind?"

Bob replies, "I think White Wonders because they are meaty and sweet. Do you like tomatoes?"

First man says "Yes, but I prefer a tarter tomato."

Bob says, "Then I suggest you try the Green Zebra."

While this need not be an important conversation, understanding how interactive conversations work will be particularly important later when discussing emotional issues. Remember to use other communication skills like saying "I" when it is a statement that you own. Start.

Let this run five minutes or until the energy starts to fade. Hold the discussion until the end of the next exercise.

Part 4: No Words

Say: *Just look into the other man's eyes. No words. Just sit. We generally find this to be "uncomfortable silence" but we will learn to overcome this barrier and simply be together without a need to talk. Again, no words, just try to be present and aware of the other man.*

Wait three full minutes then,

Say: *Stop.*

Then bring the group back together again and talk about how it felt without words, with words, how difficult it can be to listen and understand.

This is a good time to take a break.

Second Exercise: Reflective Listening

Say: *Now we are going to acquire a listening tool called reflective listening that we will often use in the group, particularly when conflicts arise or emotions are high. It is also very useful in your life outside of the group.*

In most conversations, there is distortion. A man might hear something differently than it was intended by the speaker. That's because we bring our own thinking or interpretations to the conversation as well as our own emotions. Reflective listening is simply saying back to the person what you think you heard him say; therefore, giving a man an opportu-

nity to correct any misinterpretation of what he meant. It sounds easy, but it is not. For this exercise, form into groups of three, if possible.

Say: *In this exercise one man will start. We will call him the sender. He will say something about himself to another man, more than a sentence but not more than three or four sentences. The man he says it to, we will call the receiver. Next the receiver will repeat back in his own words what he heard the sender say. The sender will then tell him if he is correct. The third man is the observer. He will then give feedback to both men. Sometimes the receiver misses an important point yet the sender fails to correct him. Therefore, the observer has to be sure both men are correctly performing their roles. I will not be saying switch, just keep changing until everyone has had a chance to play every role. We will take ten to fifteen minutes to do this.*

When everyone is done, re-form the group.

Ask: *Did you feel you were listening harder?*

Did you feel you were being listened to?

What is the value of practicing reflective listening?

Why might this skill be especially helpful in emotionally-charged conversations?

Remainder of the Meeting:

As the leader you now need to decide the agenda for the rest of the meeting. If time is short, it might be time to close. If men have brought up issues in the Opening Round, or at other times during the meeting that the group needs to get back to, do that. Or you might decide to continue with last week's rounds of emotional topics if you hadn't finished. If you do continue the meeting with any type of personal discussion, remember the skills you have learned. Practice repeating back what each man said before adding your reaction or advice.

Closing the Meeting

About 15 minutes before the end time of the meeting, start the Closing Round and do any closing ritual the group is using.

Give the talking stick and any other group materials to the next leader.

Congratulations on another successful meeting! Your group is beginning to bond.

My Notes

First thing I want to remember about this meeting.

_____

_____

_____

_____

_____

When did I feel the most uncomfortable at this meeting?

_____

_____

_____

_____

Can I use these listening skills in my life?

_____

_____

_____

_____

Meeting Five– Men Working

Preparing for the Meeting

Before the meeting, make sure you have a meeting place, you have sent out an email, and you have read the meeting script.

Opening the Meeting

Welcome everyone to the meeting in your own words. It is time to schedule leadership for future meetings. So draw names for the remainder of the meetings and then plan who will take the next twelve to twenty meetings. Every man should take approximately the same number of meetings. It is generally a good idea to schedule leadership every three to six months. Our group does it by the season - fall, winter, spring, and summer.

Next, introduce the topics. There are two major items woven together in this meeting, "Feedback" and "Work." Feedback is the reaction to what has been said. It is more than just reflecting back; it is interpreting what was said and then offering advice, challenge, or support.

Work occurs when one member wants to "work" on an issue that is troubling him; that is, a personal issue he wants to share with the group. This may have already occurred during these first meetings, but now we are going to formalize the opportunity for Work within the context of every meeting.

Opening Round

Open as normal. A suggestion for a Query is "What has been most on your mind this week?"

First Exercise: Feedback

Say: *We will continue with building our communication skills by introducing "feedback" at this meeting. It's important we learn to give safe and useful feedback. Some of the techniques that we have learned in normal society are not useful in this group. The use of sarcasm, clever jibes, or other practices designed to bolster our own self-esteem, rather than to help other members, have no place in a safe environment. That does not mean that challenging what is said isn't legitimate feedback. However, all feedback must be done in the context of facilitating. Be particularly cautious of supportive feedback. Sometimes it is not helpful. Sometimes, we give supportive feedback as a reflexive reaction because we want to be liked. Give supportive feedback only if you believe the man is on the right track. Sometimes, questioning or challenging his line of thought is better. This can be done by asking the deeper questions that cause the man to probe beyond the surface. For example, a man with a good income is faced with a pay reduction. He plans to make up the loss by getting a part-time night job as a bartender. But deeper questions might be, "I can see that this is a very painful situation for you and I am aware that you are extremely distraught. But I ask you to consider why this is such an intense issue. What are you most afraid will happen? Have you told your family and what was their reaction? How do you think this will affect your personal happiness? Or, how do you think less income will affect your relationships with your friends and family? Instead of simply seeking a solution to a perceived problem, sometimes gaining a deeper understanding of the issues results in a better outcome. In this case, a lower salary might actually result in more happiness. The man may come to understand that the most important aspects of his life are independent of money. Therefore, he may decide against the second job. If everyone in the group had simply been supportive and told him what a hard worker he was and how much they admired his willingness to sacrifice himself, he might not have considered living with a lower income. In this case, the man might, after reflection, still take the second job, but now he is more aware as to why.*

One of the best ways to keep yourself on track when giving feedback is to first reflect what was said, then add your feedback. For example, "I heard you say that you are deep in debt and this has caused you extreme anxiety, particularly because you are planning a vacation that you cannot afford. Are you more afraid of the debt or asking your family to cancel the vacation? Why do you feel this way?" In this example, you are suggesting that the man weigh the consequences of his options. You are not imposing your values on him. He may be confronted with a belief that his children and wife will not love him if they don't go to Disney World. The right feedback, provided without judgment, can often help a man verbalize what he may already know intuitively. One of the goals of feedback is to align our awareness. Ideally, our sensations (physical data that we perceive), intuition (our internal knowing), our thinking (interpretation of the information), and our emotions (feelings) should be aligned. When one of them is severely out of whack, we cannot have an awareness of the true picture. We then make choices that result in continued internal discord.

Feedback is not only given during Work but anytime during a meeting. It need not be in a formal setting. But whether or not it is during work, try to adhere to the following guidelines.

Read or ask some to read the following.

Guidelines for Giving Feedback

1. Only give feedback when requested to do so, or by first asking. (The person receiving the feedback must be in control.)

2. Always speak with caring and respect. Never use judgmental words like "stupid" or "ridiculous;" these are not useful in helping another man understand his situation.

3. Focus on behavior, not motive. For example, "I heard you say that you buy lottery tickets that you can't afford because you feel hopeless. How do you think you would feel if, for one week, you gave the money that you spend on tickets to a charity or to someone you know who is in need?"

4. Express yourself. Don't impute feelings to other. For example, a man might say, "I noticed that you haven't said anything during the meeting, and I want to tell you that I am feeling anxious and concerned," rather than saying, "You're really depressed tonight."

5. Share the effect of an observation. Say, "When I heard you raise your voice and saw your hand make a fist, I felt scared because I believed that I might be hurt."

6. Never attack the man's character; provide honest information as you understand it. Be immediate. If something happens, don't wait until the next meeting, or the following month. Give feedback at once. For example, say, "When I hear you cutting Bob off in a conversation, I feel sad because I believe that you don't value the guidelines of the group."

Some of these guidelines may look like other exercises that we have done; indeed, they are.

Have a short discussion if needed, and then read or ask someone to read the following.

Guidelines for Receiving Feedback

1. Accept feedback as being sincerely given.

2. Wait before you reply. Let the feedback sink in.

3. You are under no obligation to reply.

4. Reflect back the feedback so that you're sure you understand it, and if you're not sure what was said, ask for clarification.

5. Remember that sometimes feedback has more to do with the giver's experiences than yours. If you don't intuitively agree, you can simply dismiss it.

6. You don't have to do anything about it. It was given to you. You have no obligation to follow any advice or accept anyone's interpretation of your behavior.

7. Don't be overwhelmed. If you're getting too much feedback simply say, "Ok, that is enough."

Say: *Form into pairs; as always, try to choose someone you haven't worked with before.*

If there is an odd number, form one group of three. Wait for the groups to form.

Say: *This is again an extension of what we have been doing.*

One man says to the other: "I give you permission to tell me something that I should know about myself (feedback)." The second man replies with feedback about something that the first man does. The first man then reflects the feedback as given and thanks the man for it. Go back and forth several times. Tell the man a real observation. This is the time to start being honest. For example, if he wears too much cologne, tell him. Who else will?

For example:

The first man says, "Bob, I give you permission to tell me something about myself."

The second man responds, "I think you should know that when you roll your eyes while I am speaking, your action makes me feel devalued."

The first man reflects, "You're mad at me because I don't like what you say. Thank you for telling me."

The second man corrects, "No, I said I felt devalued, not mad. I did not say anything about you not liking what I said. My devaluation came from my interpretation of your actions, not your disagreement."

The first man then tries again to accurately reflect until the second man responds affirmatively.

The best feedback is always the hardest to give. Let's start and remember first to give permission, then feedback, then reflect the feedback, then affirm or correct the reflection.

After about 10 to 15 minutes,

Say: *Stop*

Call the circle back together.

Ask: *Was it hard to be honest even after being given permission? Was it more difficult to receive feedback or to give it?*

This might be a good place for a break.

Start this second exercise only if you have at least an hour or more remaining; otherwise move it to the next week. If you have to move it, fill in with items left undone from prior meetings or fill in with Query Rounds.

Second Exercise: Work

Say: *Work is an important part of this group. By "Work" we mean setting aside time for an individual man to work on a specific issue that is troubling him, or that he wants to share in some way.*

Work goes like this. One man is given the floor and is handed the talking stick. No one can interrupt him unless he gives permission. He starts by saying what he wants from the group. Typically, the choices are:

1. *I want to be heard without feedback or solutions. I just want to tell my story.*

2. *All feedback is welcomed.*

3. *I want only advice or suggestions.*

4. *I want to be challenged or supported so that I can come to a better understanding of what I'm saying.*

Then the man tells his story. When he is done, he says: "I'm ready for feedback." Remember he does not have to reply to feedback or to follow it. But it must be given honestly and intended for his benefit.

In order for the meeting to run smoothly, the leader will ask at the beginning of each meeting if anyone wants to work. During the Opening Round next week this additional statement will be added. "If I were to work at this meeting, it would be on____." Remember, the Opening Round is not a time to work. It is for a short check-in. Also, any man can simply pass if he is not ready to announce the topic that is troubling him.

Here is a great way to set priorities for work. It might sound a bit odd, but we have done groups with and without this technique, and it works. We will call this technique the Blind Hand Raise. After the Opening Round is done, ask every man, including the leader, to close his eyes and put up from zero to five fingers. Five fingers means that a man has very pressing issues that he wants to work on. One finger indicates there is something that he wants to bring up but the need isn't pressing. For example, if a man's partner left him that morning, it's probably a five. If he had a dispute with the cable company over the game not being broadcast, it might be a one. A closed hand (no fingers) means you have decided that there is nothing you want to work on tonight. After everyone has his hand raised, eyes are opened. The leader then asks each man showing figures how much time they think they will need. The leader then decides what to do. He may proceed with his agenda, making sure to leave time at the end for work. He may decide to do work first. If one guy only needs three minutes and another guy needs twenty, maybe the one with the shorter time goes first even if it is a less important issue. Or, maybe the most important five-finger issue goes first and then, if there isn't time, the "one" is asked to be moved to the next week. If a man has asked for twenty minutes and he is going over his time, the leader has an obligation to the group. He can either ask the group if they want to eliminate some activity, he can ask another man if he will postpone his "Work," to the next meeting, or he can tell the man working that he is at the time limit that he requested and that the meeting needs to move on.

We are now going to practice this. We will do a round saying "If I we were going to work at this meeting, I would work on (blank)." Then we are going to do the blind hand, and if anyone wants to work we will do the group's first official "Work." Ready? Let's start.

As always with rounds, pass the stick in either direction or start yourself.

Say: *I am hearing that there are some issues that men might want to work on. Okay close your eyes and hold up from zero to five fingers. "Zero" means you do not want to work tonight, and "five" means it's essential that you work.*

Open your eyes and ask how much time each man with fingers up needs. Look at the time and decide how you will divide the remaining time of the meeting. Meetings should end on time. If a man has indicated that he wants to work, hand him the stick and ask him to begin by first announcing what he wants from the group. Watch the feedback, and make sure he is making "I" statements. Correct anyone not using the communication skills that were taught in previous sessions.

If no one wants to work, fill in with an unfinished exercise or informational rounds, or start a discussion on any topic you wish.

Why no one is "working" might be a good topic.

Closing

About 15 minutes before the ending time of the meeting bring work to an end. Recognize anyone who wanted to work but wasn't able to and ask them to again bring it up at the next meeting, then start the closing round.

Give the talking stick and any other group materials to the next leader and if you have adopted a closing ritual, do it.

Congratulations on the completion of your fifth meeting!

My Notes

What are my feelings about this meeting?

_____

_____

_____

_____

_____

_____

_____

_____

What do I want to remember about this meeting?

_____

_____

_____

_____

_____

What did I learn new?

_____

_____

_____

_____

What do I want to work on over the next weeks?

_____

_____

_____

_____

_____

Meeting Six– Risky Business

Preparing for the Meeting

Before the meeting, make sure you have a meeting place, have sent out an email, and have read the meeting script. Because this is likely to be a difficult meeting for some men, you might suggest in your email that everyone read through the meeting agenda.

Opening the Meeting

The routine is setting in now. Most likely, there will be some men who will want to start working, to begin to share their story, and seek advice. Some may have been wanting to for a while and weren't sure how. These last meetings will begin to mimic typical meetings; however, there are still a few risky things to do. In this meeting, we will be given two quickie tools to help the group and then you will learn to give and to receive uncomfortable information.

Opening Round

Always keep the Opening Round short and pass the talking stick. The leader can always include a Query related or unrelated to the meeting. A work statement will be included at this meeting. I suggest including it in all future meetings.

Say: *We are at our sixth meeting; we will begin with our Opening Round. The Query for this meeting is: "_____?" And remember to include the work statement. If I were going to work tonight, it would be on._____.*

Next, do the Blind Hand Raise where every man puts up between zero and five fingers indicating the intensity of his need to work. Then announce how you're going to handle the meeting. Work first, then the exercise, or get the exercise out of the way and then work. Let the men know the order that work will happen. If there isn't enough time for everyone who wants to work, discuss whether to shorten times or postpone some work topics until next week. You also have the option of removing the exercise from the agenda.

First Exercise: Visual Tools

Tool One- "I"

Say: *We have talked a number of times about the importance of owning our statements by using "I." We have also talked about challenging men when they start to use "you," "they," "some people," or "we," when it should really be "I." Yet, we don't want to interrupt a man who has the floor. So we are going to start practicing using the American Sign Language sign for "I." With your right hand make a fist, then extend your small finger and place your hand on your left shoulder. When you hear a man not using "I" when he should, simply give him the sign. Without interruption, you can help him change in mid-sentence. Let's practice it.*

Tool Two - "O"

Say: *Sometimes the leader needs help. Sometimes one man is starting to work in the Opening Round rather than simply checking-in. Or maybe someone has asked for ten minutes and he has now run on for twenty-five. This can damage the group. But again, sometimes a man doesn't want to interrupt, thinking that the leader will take control any second. Here is another sign to silently signal the leader as soon as a boundary is broken. Simply make an "O" with your right hand using your thumb and fingers. Your thumb tip should rest between your pointer and index finger. Let's practice it.*

Second Exercise: Risky Feedback

Say: *This exercise is designed to make everyone uncomfortable, perhaps even a bit wounded, so that you can practice healing. Men who can't absorb criticism or discomfort will leave the group soon anyway because they lack the ability to withstand any perceived attack on their self-esteem. Unfortunately in society, there are many men who run at the first moment of discord or conflict. Doing so, they fail to reap the rewards of truly bonded kinship.*

Even more difficult than receiving a painful comment is giving uncomfortable feedback. Speaking means being accountable and many men have never learned to take responsibility. Even when we know we are

*speaking for the benefit of the other man, we may be so fearful of be-
ing misunderstood, or of being disliked, that we remain silent or make
a meaningless watered-down statement. Remember the tools that we
have learned. By asking the man to reflect back what you said, you
can be sure he understood what you meant, and have the opportunity
to correct it if it was incorrectly perceived. It is often helpful to start
difficult comments by first stating that what you are saying is based on
your perceptions of what you see, hear, feel, or intuitively understand,
and are grounded solely on your knowledge and your experiences.*

*For the group to bond and to be beneficial, it must be a place where
everyone is free to say anything without fear of the consequences, a
place where openness and honesty trump fear. Therefore it is the responsibility of every man to help each other say difficult things. There
is nothing as poisonous as "the elephant in the room" that everyone is
afraid to mention.*

*I hope everyone here understands that we are practicing some riskier
behaviors tonight. It is not the purpose of this exercise to alienate anyone. The purpose is to give everyone feedback on their perceptions,
perceptions that are understood by all to be imperfect and often incor-
rect. It is an exercise in both giving and receiving, and in correcting
misconceptions.*

*In designing this exercise, the manual's author does understand that he
created an artificial issue with concerns that are most likely unfounded.
However, he needed to design this exercise in a way that works for all
groups. There may be issues within our group that will require even
more frankness. If a man has an issue with the group, anything that
happened in the group or between group members, requesting work
time is a great way to resolve it.*

*Let's begin. Look around the group and decide in your own mind who
you are most concerned will leave the group. You can't dodge the question by saying that you are confident that every man will stay. Naming
someone doesn't mean that you want him to leave; just the opposite
might be true. Once you have picked your man, do not change your
mind no matter what. Next pick the man you think is least likely to
leave. Don't play games here. You might be tempted to pick the man
that you think everyone thinks might leave, as the guy you think will*

stay, just to encourage him to remain. Honesty is what we are practicing, not manipulation!

Give it a minute and then start a round where each man will announce both his picks and then tell why. The man receiving the feedback can reflect the feedback to insure that he understands it and he can ask clarifying questions. Remember, the feedback is honestly given as the giver's observation and his sincerity cannot be questioned.

This exercise is particularly difficult if the same man is picked by everyone. If this happens, the man chosen will now understand the messages his verbal cues or body-language communicate. Understanding how you are coming across can be life changing. I know of one man's life that completely changed for the better, after another man was courageous enough to talk to him about his communication skills.

Take one minute to think, and then start.

This round may take a while. Keep going until everyone is done. You can do the next exercise at another meeting if you need to.

After this round is over, it might be a good time to take a break.

Third Exercise: Truth Telling

Say: *We are now going to do another difficult round. We will talk about the group's confidentiality. Sometimes breaks happen. This can be easy to do, depending on where the boundaries have been set. Small leaks occur. For example, a man might tell his wife, "Gosh, Bill lost his job, I felt so bad for him." Then he realizes that, again depending on what the group has decided is confidential, he has crossed the line. Perhaps he only said, "One of the guys lost his job," and thought that was acceptable because he didn't mention the man's name. Bill may not agree.*

Or, maybe, when telling a friend about the group, the friend asked, "What kind of things do the guys talk about there?" In giving his reply, he may have used examples that crossed the line.

Or one of the men may have said something to you like, "When I told my wife that you lost your job, she suggested that you call Mr. Smith at her office because they are hiring in your field." Did you think he crossed the line, but also knew that he was trying to be helpful? Did you tell him how you felt? If not, now is the time to tell him how you feel. Express your understanding of his actions but also make it clear that you felt the line was crossed. Saying it is harder than hearing it, but honest communications are needed or the group will not grow.

We might also want to review our earlier decisions on what is confidential; we may want to change it, but only if we have 100% agreement. Remember, if a man did mess up, that fact stays in the group. Let's make sure we remember our communication tools for working through a conflict if any occur. Talking about it now will hurt, but it will also build the group stronger.

After a minute for each man to think this over, start the round.

Follow with any discussion that is needed.

Remainder of Meeting

If you worked first, you're most likely at the end of the meeting. If you waited, then now is the time for work.

Closing

About fifteen minutes before the end of the meeting, bring work to an end. Recognize anyone who wanted to work but wasn't able to and ask them to please bring it up at the next meeting.

Announce that next week's meeting will be about play. Ask the men to read though the entire next meeting during the week.

Start the closing round. Remember, the round is "How are you feeling right now, and is there any unfinished business?" Then, do any closing ritual the group has decided on. Remember that new rituals can be introduced at any time and old ones removed when they no longer meet the group's needs.

Congratulations on completing a difficult meeting!

My Notes

What are my feelings about this meeting?

_____

_____

_____

_____

_____

_____

What do I want to remember, what new thing did I learn?

_____

_____

_____

_____

_____

Am I glad that I have this group of men?

_____

_____

_____

_____

_____

Meeting Seven – Let's Play

Preparing for the Meeting

Before the meeting, read through all the meeting instructions; in particular, understand the safety rules for play. Select the games you want to play. Get everything together that you need. If you are planning games where boundaries need to be marked, do that ahead of time if you can. Ask one of the men to come early to help you. It is best to write down the order of the games.

When you contact the men with a reminder of the location, let the men know what is planned so that they can dress appropriately or bring a change of clothing and include a reminder for them to read the contents of meeting seven. In particular, it is important that they read the following articles: "Men Playing," "Rules for Good Safe Play," and "The Real Winner."

Men Playing

Play is different from competitive activities. I know they say sports are not about winning or losing, but how you play the game. But if that's true, why do they keep score? I'm not downgrading sports. Sports have an ability to build many positive character traits. They are enjoyable to play and a thrill to watch. Sometimes they are fun, sometimes they are not. On the other hand, play is always fun. And the camaraderie of play will always build friendships and bond a group. Men instinctively like to play, but it is something that society tries to extinguish in us. Think about school. How many times did you hear "Stop horsing around," or "Stop goofing off"? In school, participation in sports was praised and celebrated at pep rallies, and academic success was recognized on the Dean's List. However, no one rewarded the guy who inspired the students to play during class. And think about this: the fun person motivating the play was almost always a male. Play is one of the most masculine traits we have, and it is the one male trait that society most tries to subvert or eliminate.

Back in the 1970's, my wife and I took a training course with the emerging New Games Foundation. For me, it was an eye opener to the fun of play. Adults played Tag, Blob, Vampire, Knots, and Samurai Warrior.

The New Games Foundation is still a great source for ideas. Their web site is www.inewgames.com. They state on their site:

> "Through the games we play and the way we play them, we encourage participation, creativity, and personal expression. The playful spirit is free to emerge from within. As partners rather than opponents, we compete against the limits of our own abilities instead of against each other. Ultimately, in playing together, we learn to live together."

I was told that the New Games Foundation started as a result of a peace demonstration. At the demonstration, a large ball was painted like an earth globe. The speaker said that there are two kinds of people in the world: those that want to push the world over that edge in one direction and those that want to push it off the other end. To demonstrate this, participants started pushing the big ball. But as it turned out, they were having so much fun that everyone started joining in, and then a strange thing happened. When one team was about to win, people changed sides. Having fun was more important than winning. The game went on for hours, with the participants laughing, getting dirty, sweating, smiling, and becoming aware that fun is an important part of our life.

Rules for Good Safe Play

The cardinal rules of New Games have not changed since I was trained. They should be adopted and reviewed by every men's group every time before beginning play. Paraphrased they are: Play Hard, Play Fair and Nobody Gets Hurt.

1. **Play Hard.** Everyone participates fully: You are among friends. There is no one to impress. Don't worry about your performance. This is uninhibited play, not sport. So, put your heart and soul into the moment.

2. **Play Fair.** This isn't about winning. The goal is fun. If you're playing tag and the guy gets you, don't argue about it. It takes the fun away for you and for him. If you're told you crossed the line, accept it and accept that everyone is playing fairly. Cheating in play cheats everyone.

3. **Nobody Gets Hurt.** Sure, it's all fun and games until an eye gets put out. Or even until one of the guys gets a bit put out. Be careful because men can get carried away. Here is a good rule to follow: For any reason, a man can stop the game. If he is hurt, going to throw-up, tired, lost his contact lens, or just wants to stop, he says "Stop." Whoever hears him, starts repeating "stop," until everyone has stopped. This does two things. First, it helps to spread the word to stop, and second, it supports him in his call to stop. He is not the only one yelling stop.

Remember hurt can also be emotional, so don't insult anyone or don't make a guy feel bad. This is fun. In play, men should not be punished for having fun.

Optional Rules Here are two optional rules to consider at the start of every game. Sometimes they make sense sometimes not. They can make some games fair, fun, and over the top.

1. Anyone can switch sides anytime they want. This is a great way to play a lot of games. It takes the importance out of whose team is better. It is especially fun to switch to the side that's losing because it's more fun to be the underdog.

2. If it is a game where a score is kept, let the guy scoring decide how much his success is worth.

I once played basketball this way, and made a shot worth 10,000 points. That was a tenfold increase over their previous 1,000-point baskets. Point inflation was out of control, and with nine guys on each team, sometimes the play was as well. (Well, that's how it started, but sometimes it was fifteen guys against three guys.) With the score and the play out of control, so was the fun. With my 10,000 point shot, we would have won, but then the other team retroactively made their first basket worth a million points, wiping us out. We didn't see that one coming, so we all retroactively switched to their side. Best basketball game I ever played.

I think you get the idea. Decide whatever rules you want and then play for fun, play for fairness, and play for the sake of playing.

The Real Winner

When I was trained in New Games, one of the men in our group was a high school physical education teacher in his late twenties. He was in exceptional condition, the epitome of an excellent athlete. I knew intuitively that he could beat everyone there in any game we played. But as it turned out, he was the biggest loser of the weekend. The contempt he had for just having fun was visible in his every gesture. He didn't "play." He participated, but he was always striving to maintain his athletic posture and dignity. By the start of the second day, he was gone. He couldn't do it. He couldn't bring himself to play. On the other hand, a visibly out of shape middle-aged woman caught on and had more fun in those two days than she had had in years. She announced that she had also exercised more than she had in years. She was the biggest winner; she found she could have fun.

Planning Your Games

At this meeting, I hope everyone will have fun. I have given the rules for a few games, but please play any game or fun activity you want to do. If you can go to a park, or someone has a big back yard, you can do big movement and running games. Otherwise, if you are indoors and can't spread out, do word games, board games (Monopoly where cheating is permitted but with jail time if caught), card games, tell jokes, sing goofy camp songs, or anything playful.

Opening the Meeting

Welcome everyone, do the Opening Round, Blind Hand Raise, work if needed, or hold off until the end. You as the leader can also decide and announce at the beginning of the meeting that the agenda is full so only men with a level five need will work at this meeting. That way, if a guy really has an issue, he has an opportunity to work, while at the same time letting everyone know you have a lot planned.

Ask if everyone has read though the meeting materials. If anyone was not able to get through it, then read aloud, "Men Playing," "Rules for Good Safe Play," and "The Real Winner."

First Exercise: Play

Say: *Tonight we are going to play. Three rules about play are Play Hard, Play Fair, and Nobody Gets Hurt.*

In your own words, review what you mean by the three rules or read from above. And then introduce the play.

Play any of the games listed below or use any game or activity you want.

Knots

Form a circle; everyone randomly joins hands (across from you, beside you, behind you). Mix it up real good to form a human knot. Now try to untie the knot without letting go. You should be able to form a circle by moving under and around each other. Some guys might be facing out and some in. Maybe you end up with two circles. Try it and see.

Freeze Tag

One man is "It." If he touches another man, that man must not move unless another player touches him. The game ends when everyone is "frozen."

Dragon's Jewels

Use any small object that's easy to grab. A sock tied in a knot or a bean bag works well. One man is the dragon. He is the guardian of the jewels. He places the jewels on the ground and stands over them, not on them. He may not touch the jewels or move them in anyway. He says, "Go," and everyone tries to grab the jewels. If he tags you, you're "frozen" until the next round. The round ends when everyone is frozen or when someone gets the jewels away from the guardian. (Hint: sneak up from behind.) Whoever gets the jewels is the Guardian Dragon of the next round.

Vampire

Play this at night if you can. You need complete darkness, blindfolds, or just close your eyes tight. One man is the vampire. Blindly walk around. If the vampire grabs you, he will scream. You are now a vampire, too. Now you both wander about trying to get new victims. If a vampire grabs another vampire, you both scream. If this happens the spell is broken and you are both freed from the vampire curse. But be careful, you have already created vampires who will now get you. The game ends when everyone is a vampire or until everyone is free from the vampire curse.

Moon Light, Star Light

This is tag in reverse with a theme. It is best played at night in the woods, desert, or a large building with low lighting. One man is the ghost. He hides while the other men, with eyes closed, stand by the "Goal" counting. The goal can be a tree, rock, door, table or anything. The count is by o'clock: one o'clock, two o'clock, three o'clock … up to twelve. Then the men spread out looking for the ghost chanting, "Moon light, star light, hope to see a ghost tonight, one o'clock the ghost not here, two o'clock the ghost not here" etc.… up to twelve and then starting over. At some point, the ghost jumps out and chases everyone. Once the ghost appears, everyone runs for the goal. If they make it, they are safe. If a man is tagged by the ghost, then he becomes the next ghost for the next round. If everyone reaches the goal, then the same guy is the ghost.

Stumps

This is an old medieval game. Two men squat down standing on a short stump (box, foot stool, whatever) that are placed six to eight feet apart. They hold a rope that is about four feet longer than the distance between the stumps. By pulling on the rope or relaxing the tension on the rope while the other guy is pulling, each man tries to get the other off his stump.

Slaughter

This game is not for everyone. If you play it, be safe. Take your shoes off and draw a circle or some shape on the ground big enough to accommodate all the players with their arms out. Indoors, tape works well; outdoors, chalk, rope, or even string works. All the men get in the circle on their hands and knees. When the leader says, "Go," it's a free for all. Everyone tries to push, roll, and toss everyone else out of the circle until only one guy is left. If any part of a guy, (his hand, foot, etc.) is out, and touching the ground, he is out. You may not stand up but you can use your hands, legs, feet, and torso to get the other guys out. There is always confusion on this one, so play fair. If a man saw your little finger touch the ground outside the circle, it did. You're out! Also, keep the "Stop" rule clear. This one can be a bit rough. You can make up lot of variations of this game (including playing it standing). It's kind of like King of the Hill, but with, we hope, fewer broken arms. Be very careful that everyone is physically fit to play, and that no one gets hurt.

Other Games

Think of any childhood game to play, look on the internet or add new twists to an old one. There are many variations of Kick the Can, Tag, and Hide-and-Seek. We once played a game called Samurai Warrior based on the Saturday Night Live characters. It was such an odd twist on "Duck, Duck, Goose" that we could never stop laughing long enough to finish.

Remember to take a break at some time.

Second Exercise: Homework Assignment

Say: *The next meeting is our eighth. At this meeting we will be evaluating ourselves and the group. In the notes section after this meeting is a list of items each of us needs to think about before the next meeting. Please fill in whatever you think is important before we meet again.*

Closing

You know what to do.

Congratulations! You had fun and you are almost to the eighth meeting.

My Notes and Home Work

Notes

Was play fun for me?

_____

_____

How can I play more in my life?

_____

_____

_____

_____

_____

Homework for Meeting Eight

What does being a "Men's Group" mean?

_____

_____

_____

_____

_____

_____

_____

_____

How much can I trust these men?

_____

_____

_____

_____

_____

Do I want to remain with this group?

_____

_____

_____

_____

_____

Have my goals been met?

(Look at the goals you wrote down early on.)

_____

_____

_____

_____

_____

What are my goals for the long term?

_____

_____

_____

_____

_____

What are my goals for the group over the next year?

_____

_____

_____

_____

_____

Have my goals changed?

_____

_____

Do I think all the members participated openly and honestly in all the activities?

_____

_____

_____

_____

_____

How is the group functioning as a community?

_____

_____

_____

_____

_____

_____

_____

_____

Is there anything holding me back from forming a closer bond with these men? If so what is it?

_____

_____

_____

_____

_____

_____

To what extent is the group using the communication skills we have learned?

_____

_____

_____

_____

_____

Is communication open and honest all the time? Have I held back saying something because I was afraid of hurting someone or of being rejected? Is there anything I need to say before moving on? (This is important. By saying it, your relationship can heal, otherwise in the back of your mind it will always be something that you wanted to say.)

_____

_____

_____

_____

_____

_____

_____

Is there something that needs to be changed in the group? If so, what is it?

_____

_____

_____

_____

_____

What might be hindering the group from being a community?

_____

_____

_____

_____

_____

What meeting did I enjoy the most?

_____

_____

_____

_____

Do I consider these men friends?

_____

_____

_____

_____

_____

Am I ready to take responsibility for my group?

_____

_____

_____

_____

_____

Meeting Eight– Looking Forward

Preparing for the Meeting

Before the meeting, you might want to send out an email reminding everyone to fill out their responses to the questions, and have yours prepared, too. Read through this chapter. For this meeting you might want to abandon my scripting and just speak in your own words.

Opening the Meeting

Welcome, congratulate everyone, and introduce the meeting's topic.

Opening Round

(Check in, Query and Work)

Blind Hand Show

(Zero to Five fingers)

First Exercise: Evaluation

Where have we been?
Where are we now?
What do we want to change?

Say: *This meeting is an evaluation of the group and every man's place in it. In addition to the "Home Work" questions feel free to ask other questions about the group. There is a lot to talk about. If we don't finish everything, we will just continue next week or at a later meeting.*

As we discuss the past eight meetings and where we are now, include your experiences based on what you physically observe, know intuitively, intellectually understand, and most importantly, be aware of how your feelings have changed.

Let's start with the most important question, the first question; "What does being a Men's Group mean?"

If you finish that one, continue with the other questions.

Second Exercise: Friendships Outside of the Meeting

Say: *"Are we friends, a group, or both?" Your group members may have already started doing things with each other outside of the group. How does everyone feel about members socializing outside of the group? If two guys go to a baseball game, does everyone need to be invited? What if two guys and their partners want to go a new restaurant?*

Here is the advice the manual's author has. We can decide to follow it or reject it. This is our group, not his. He writes, "Not everyone needs to be invited everywhere. You are individuals, and there is no need to include everyone from the group in everything you do. If you are not included, there is no reason to feel jealous or rejected. Such feelings have no place among brothers. If you're fearful that such feelings might emerge in the group, you're not yet bonded. In every group some men will just have some interests in common that others don't. Never be afraid to mention things you did with other members that didn't include everyone. Each member should feel secure that his worth as a bona fide member of the group is never threatened or devalued. If, however, you do feel rejected, or uncomfortable asking someone to coffee, bring it up as work. Being able to talk about feelings, all feelings, will make you and the group stronger.

I also suggest that you make an effort to get to know the men in your group with whom you have less in common. You might agree that this month everyone is going to call someone that they haven't yet socialized with outside of the group. You might just get a cup of coffee, hike, have lunch, a beer, go to a movie, just hangout and watch a game on T.V., etc. At the very least, every man can find the time to have a phone conversation. So, make a contact. Include partners and family if you want.

For some men calling or emailing to set up something can be difficult. If it is for you, ask yourself why? You might want to bring it up as a work issue or design a meeting around it. Learning that other men have the same difficulty can help you overcome your anxiety. As time goes by, you will get used to calling each other, and doing things together will feel normal."

Let's talk about it and decide what we want to do.

In Chapters 11 and 12, I have outlined more meeting activities and rituals that can be a part of your group. One of them is called "Stretches." This activity has been a benefit to a lot of groups. In Chapter 13, I have outlined some topics for future meetings. Some are designed to bring a bit of discomfort to the group. As your group evolves, keep it fresh with injections of new activities, but never forget the communication skills you have learned. Some groups repeat the communication exercises occasionally, and also review the Laws and Guidelines periodically.

Closing

You know what to do.

Congratulations!

This is truly your group and unfortunately for me, I'm not a member. So I won't be able to join you in your adventures. Best of success to you and let us know how you are doing at www.MensGroupManual.com.

My Notes

What are my feelings about this meeting?

_____

_____

_____

_____

_____

_____

_____

Did my group decide to change anything?

_____

_____

_____

_____

_____

_____

_____

_____

_____

Chapter 11:
Other Activities

In this chapter, I will outline some meeting elements that your group may want to try. Adding new activities will help keep your group engaged and excited. They can also be easily adapted for various topics. In the next chapter, I have included elements that some groups have adopted as set activities that they use at every meeting; therefore I have classified them as rituals. However, there is a thin line between the two. You might want to try these activities for few meetings, once in a while, or use activities from this chapter at every meeting. In Chapter 13, I have put together some meeting topics. Using these three chapters together for planning may be helpful.

The Question Hat

Pass out cards and ask every man to write a question on it; no name, just a printed question. The question might deal with the theme of the meeting or be a free-for-all. You also need not limit each man to one question card. Perhaps some men are inspired to ask several questions. If you don't get to them all, you can save them for another meeting. Collect the cards either folded or face down and mix them up. Now draw one from a hat and do a round based on it.

As a variation on this, have everyone write questions as homework and then bring them to the meeting.

The round dealing with each question can be set up as a fast one sentence reply, or set up as a longer discussion. If it is a longer discussion, set up the format using the communication tools that you have learned. For example, before the man replies to the question, he announces what feedback he wants, if any. He uses "I" statements and expresses any awareness of senses, interpretation, intuition, or emotion. For example, a simple question like, "Did your dad come to your school for sport activities?" for some men can be tough. He might reply after announcing what he wants as feedback. "I am aware that I'm feeling hot; I think it is because I'm still angry that my dad never came to anything. But I know intuitively that the reason was that he couldn't overcome his fear of feeling out of place. Not even for me." This might bring feedback such as "Would it help if you talk to your father about this now, so that he understands both your emotions and your understanding?"

Because these can easily slip into work, lay out the ground rules before you start. Decide that each man can have as long as he needs, even if only one man answers the question. Or decide that every man should get a chance to reply to the question and therefore limit the time for each reply. If time is limited, talk about more time later, perhaps at the end of the meeting, or as work at the next meeting.

The Nourishment Game

One man is selected and then a round follows where every man tells him what he likes or admires about him. Either do one man a week, (names drawn from an envelope until everyone has been chosen always works well for this) or use the time at a single meeting to give everyone a turn.

A variation on this activity that is more difficult, but ultimately very nourishing, is to start out by saying the man's name and then saying what you find blocking you from feeling closer to him. For example, "Bob, every time I attempt to tell you something positive about yourself, you look away. This causes me to feel sad because I think you don't believe what I'm saying."

You can think of a lot of other variations for this activity. Remember, it is called the Nourishment Game so always be aware that the goal is to help the man.

The Bragging Game

At one time it was considered a virtue to brag. A man who was able to tell of his own accomplishments was considered a man's man. Then somehow women decided that this wasn't very gentlemanly and we were discouraged from doing so. Now, if a man wants to brag, he has to hire a publicity agent. Well heck, how about just letting loose? Each man takes about three to four minutes, (more time only if you won the Nobel Peace Prize) and unabashedly tells in the most bombastic terms what he is proud of. When the man is done, rather than the groans we have been taught to make, everyone cheers and applauds. As men, we need to once again be free to say what we are proud of, and support what our friends are proud of. For example "I am proud that when I brag, I brag without a shred of humility. I'm the best damn braggart I know."

This can be tailored to a topic. For example, "In my relationship with my father I am most proud that I __."

The Introduction Game

This can be played in a number of ways. It is a way of introducing people that are not here but who have influenced your life. For example, "I would like to introduce my dad. He was.... and our relationship was.... and I was always aware that... I feel... and so on."

You can introduce family or other influential personalities in your life. For example, "I would like you to meet Thomas Jefferson, from whom I learned...," or "Meet Frankenstein's Monster, whose story taught me..."

Role Play

Take on the personality of someone else. Again, let's use our fathers in our example and then set up a scenario; a typical family dinner, a vacation trip, or Christmas. This can be playful or it can turn dramatic. It is said that there is a thin line between comedy and tragedy, but it is also said that, when one can laugh at the pain, the healing will start. Make sure everyone wants to do it and set a time limit. Ten to fifteen minutes is good, followed with discussion.

Another way to play this is to pair up. One man plays the role of an important person in the life of the other (in our example, his father), and the other tells him everything he would want to say to him if he were able to hear it, positive or negative. This can be dramatic. Everyone can do it at once in pairs or have just two men at a time with everyone else ready to give support and feedback.

Tell and Ask Game

Each man writes his name at the top of a piece of paper. On it are two
columns. As the papers are passed around, each man writes down in
the first column something that he wants to tell the man whose name
is at the top, and in the second column he writes down something he
wants to know about him. When each man's paper gets back to him,
you are ready to begin. Someone starts by reading his own sheet. He
may choose to pass on any question. You can either do this in rounds,
where each man reads one entry from each column, or in a round where
each man reads his whole sheet before moving on. It is important that
each man think about what he is writing, and doesn't simply ask every
man the same thing.

This activity can be altered for specific themes. For example, if the
meeting was dealing with boyhood, then the questions could be specific
to those years.

Another variation is having each man write down speculations based on
observations for each other man. For example, "I think that you read
a lot because reading was valued in your home as a child." During the
round, this perception can be affirmed or corrected. This is a way of
understanding how much you know about each other.

I Am

It has been said that all philosophy and all spirituality is really just asking ourselves who we are. By doing so, we can discover everything. In
this exercise we are helped by having another man ask and hear what we
say. This is best done without any forethought. It can be done every six
months or so, because who we are changes.

Pair up. First man starts by saying "Tell me who you are."

The second man replies, "I am ..."

The first man says, "Thank you," and again asks the question, "Tell me
who you really are."

The second man replies, attempting to go deeper into his understanding of who he is, starting with "I am …."

The second man thanks him again, but asks, "Tell me who you really are beyond that."

The first man listens and thanks him. Now switch.

Minute Man

This is a more intimate approach than a circle. In this exercise men practice talking Man to Man on difficult topics.

Sometimes your meetings get to looking a bit like a therapy group with everyone sitting around in circles. Here is a way to really change that. Decide on a somewhat risky topic, for example "One thing I don't like about you is…," "My first impression of you was…," "What I don't want you to know about me is…," "What I see in you that I see in myself is…," or something related to the theme of the meeting. Next, pair up and decide who will go first. Decide whether you want feedback or just a "thank you." Then the two men switch. Form new pairs until everyone has had a chance to share his feelings with every man. If there is an odd number, this will still work if one guy sits out once and only once as the groups change.

No Return

This requires trust and at the same time builds trust. It is a type of query, but with a twist. Each man is given two small pieces of paper, two poker chips, or anything that can be concealed in one hand. On one is the word "YES," on the other, "NO." The query must be answerable with a simple yes or no. For example, "Do you ever feel totally alone in the world?" or "Do you ever feel there is no God?" Each man places the answer into his hand and holds it out. You can't change it now. Everyone opens their hand at the same time revealing their answers.

If your group wants to use this activity, any man choosing to pass must announce it before the hands are held out. It would be very damaging if some hands were empty and others were not. It is a good rule that if one man passes, skip the question and move on. Again, these can be themed for the meeting and are often a way to break the ice for a discussion of a difficult topic.

Chapter 12:
Optional Rituals

Sometimes rituals spring up spontaneously, like giving a cheer at the end of every meeting did with our group. Sometimes they require planning, agreement, and props - like notching the talking stick at the start of the meeting. If your group is acquiring props for your meetings - things like the Talking Stick, note book, extra copy of the manual, etc. -decide how these are to be kept. We use a briefcase in which everything fits nicely. The next leader gets it at the end of each meeting.

Stretches

A stretch is a personal goal or a decision to take on a challenging task that has been neglected. A man announces it to the group and records it. They can be as simple as losing 10 pounds or getting the garage cleaned out, or more complex issues like reestablishing communication with family or addressing a toxic personal relationship. The goal should have a deadline attached to it. Stretches can become part of the closing round or be a separate round in itself. Some of the best stretches are tasks to be completed before the next meeting. For example, "I will talk to my boss about a raise this week." If it is a longer term goal, how it is going to be accomplished needs to be mapped out. For example, using our simple weight loss example, a man might set the goal as an incremental weekly goal of one pound per week for ten weeks. Making these goals as behavior specific as possible will produce the highest level of results. For example, "I'm going to complement my wife at least once a day," rather than, "I'm going to improve my relationship with my wife;" or "I'm going to call my son before Friday and tell him that I'm sorry," rather than, "I'm going to work on reestablishing my relations with my family." A man is more accountable when he is held to a behavior. The more personally significant and emotionally loaded the stretch is, the

more important it will be to have the group's support and for the group
to hold the man accountable to his word. Some of your goals can also
be tied to the work you do in the group. Perhaps the outcome of a work
session is the establishment of a stretch.

After setting a stretch, it is best to write it down in a group notebook.
Keep it with the talking stick and give it to the leader. At the Closing
Round or a separate round, the leader opens the notebook and reads last
week's stretches. Another way to handle the record keeping is to have
a Keeper of the Stretches. The same man each week keeps the record.
Either way, a stretch is a way of asking the group to hold you accountable and to share and celebrate your success. Keep this positive; no
shaming if the man fails. But give him a cheer when he makes it. For
some groups, this has turned into a major ritual of the group with drum
beating and whooping it up at every accomplishment.

Drumming

Some groups drum at their meetings. Men like pounding on stuff and
making big noises. I think it is in our genetic code; it simulates the
rhythm of life. Some music theorists think it is a way of recalling our
time in utero, the sounds of our mother's heart beat intertwining with
ours. In your group, never be afraid to let the boy inside you out to play.
Some groups drum at the start of every meeting. As men arrive, they
join in. When the time is right, the leader stops them and the meeting
starts. It's a great way to transition into another kind of space and time.
Some groups close with drumming and some do it at both ends. Groups
that have made drumming an intrinsic part of their gatherings often use
their drums to add punctuation to their meetings. For example, if a man
achieved his stretch, they do a short blast of drumming. If drumming is
too loud for your meeting location but you like the idea, rattles achieve
the same purpose at lower decibels.

Other groups do drumming only at some specific meetings or not at all.

Closing Options

A group embrace where the men form a huddle is a very common closing. Moving this up a notch you can add making eye contact with each

man during the hug. This is a way of recognizing each man on a personal level and simultaneously as a member of your group.

Other groups do the hand-pile cheer. Everyone puts one hand in, and then they give a cheer as their hands are raised. A variation is the fist-bump or your group can get very elaborate with a series of secret movements symbolizing aspects of your group. Either decide on rituals or let them evolve naturally.

Prayer

Many groups, particularly faith-based groups, open and close with prayers and accent may parts of their meetings with expressions of faith. For example, before a man works, he prays that he is given the strength to be honest and open and that the group will not betray his trust. A "Thanks be to God," punctuates a man achieving a stretch.

For groups with a less of a specific faith base, but with strong spiritual purpose, generic prayers are often decided on, or written by the group.

In some ecumenical groups, one man is asked each week to start the meeting with a prayer or reading from his faith.

Readings

Some groups use part of each meeting to work on discussions of a specific reading or even work through an entire book chapter-by-chapter. Men relate the readings to their personal lives and are aware of the emotional impact that it may have.

For faith-based groups, working their way through the Koran, Bible, Vedas, or other texts is a means to incorporate their faith as part of the group. If you choose to do so, this should vary from the traditional Bible study class, in that it is important to discuss what the text means to each man, how its words are interpreted emotionally and intuitively, rather than understanding it only from a historical or theological perspective.

Singing

Men singing in harmony is a great sound. If you incorporate music as an opener, closer, or accent to the meeting, it is really important that every man feels comfortable singing or not singing. If you want singing to be a requirement of your group, you should have that in the posting for the group and make clear during the interview the level of skill that you expect.

Food and Drink

Some groups include food and drink. At break time, the leader might serve cookies or pie. Some groups have wine, cheese or snacks after each meeting as a social time together, others coffee and doughnuts. If your group is coming from various locations after work to meet, dinner together before the meeting might be a good idea. Food and drink are a great way to bond a group.

If alcohol is part of your meeting, talk about it first. Intoxication during a meeting might feel like bonding but it really isn't. Keep alcohol light at least until after the meeting. Sometimes groups also go out for a drink afterwards. That can be a good time and a way of seeing each other in a different environment.

Play

One of the first eight meetings was devoted to play. Some groups reserve time at every meeting to do something silly that they would not do in their normal life. It might be starting with a silly song (either one the group wrote or one they know) or some kind of game.

One way of incorporating a game is to use it as a transition to the meeting. For example, a game of Frisbee tag or Frisbee golf might begin a half hour or more before the meeting. Men join in when they get there. The meeting starts when the game is over. This works well if men are coming from work and arrive at different times and if the game allows new players to be integrated easily.

Introducing and Changing Rituals

If you want to add or change a ritual, announce it as a topic of work. Then express your reasons and ask for feedback. Be honest. If you feel that you don't want to give up time for a new ritual, or feel that an existing ritual is still meaningful, say so. Groups, like people, tend to be more flexible when they are young, so consider some of these rituals early on. If everyone agrees, try it. It shouldn't be a big deal to change it again.

Some of the activities and rituals outlined in this chapter might become part of every meeting, some planned at intervals through-out the year, and others never attempted. Always be open to change but don't force the group to move in directions that intuitively don't feel right. Nothing is so sad as a group of guys trying to drum every week who hate doing it. Everything in your group needs to be nourished with the life force of the men, so keep it alive and healthy. On the website www.MensGroupManual.com under the **Sharing Information** menu are more activities and rituals. If you have suggestions for others, please share your ideas.

Notes: What do I want to try as a ritual?

_____

_____

_____

_____

_____

Chapter 13:
Meeting Topics

This alphabetical list is not exhaustive by any means. If you are looking for more ideas, or have had a particularly good meeting and want to share it, please do. Look on the website www.MensGroupManual.com under the **Sharing Information** menu for the **Meeting Topics** page. We are looking forward to hearing from you.

On some of the topics below, I have included some suggestions, questions, and information. However, this is your group, not mine, so don't feel obligated to include anything that I suggest.

Aging

This is a particularly wonderful meeting if you have a wide variety of ages in your group. Men in their late thirties can ask a man in his seventies what to expect. The fears of aging can be eased. There have been some insightful studies done on aging. One publication that is exceptionally well done is <u>Aging Well</u> by George E. Vaillant, M.D. I recommend reading it if you are running this meeting so you can bring in some of the information from the studies quoted. Based on the research, being part of social organizations like a men's group may be one of the best steps you can take to shape a happy future.

Brain Storm

Everyone tosses out ideas for future meetings. After some discussion about what each meeting could include, each man volunteers to take one of the meetings. If some topics aren't picked, don't do them. On the other hand, if the group decides on a certain set of meetings, you could draw names to determine leaders. Drawing names always works particularly well when the group has identified a difficult topic that is important to address. If you come up with some good ones, share them with us on the website.

Conflicts

Do we avoid conflicts at all cost? What are the results of facing conflicts and what are the costs of dodging them? How do we decide when to engage in conflict? This is where some role-playing games work well. For example, one man plays the mother-in-law and another practices using all the communication skills he has learned. After about ten minutes, they stop and the other men in the group give feedback. Then they switch roles for the next round.

Men need to practice conflict in order to be comfortable with it. Knights spent years in role-playing and practicing combat just to be ready for a few crucial minutes of their lives. Some of our non-physical conflicts can be as important. As men in community, we can help strengthen and prepare our comrades to do battle.

Crafts

For groups that include drumming, this is a great meeting. Men can make rattles, shakers, clackers, or decorate their drums. Other groups can make posters, cards, or decorate a small wooden craft box. In ancient times, men worked together for hours. Some of the oldest archeological digs have revealed rows of flint-chip piles. It is believed that they were made by men sitting in a row making spear heads. One theory is that music started by the men chipping flint in rhythm as they worked in huts.

Death

We are all going to do it one day and we all have thought about it. Is there an afterlife? Is death just a part of a continuing cycle of reincarnation? How would we prefer to die? Would it be better to know a year in advance or go in a flash? What about writing a bucket list? (Things we want to do before we kick the bucket.) How and why do some men avoid accepting the inevitability of death while others easily accept it? Why do some men die spiritually before they die physically?

Delayed Gratification

In one study, preschoolers were brought into a room with several M&M's on the table. They were told that they would be left alone for a while (no time was given) and that, if they wanted to, they could eat the M&M's. But if they waited without eating them until the adult returned, they would be given more (again, no amount was indicated). After the experiment was finished, the children were then tracked for many years. The children who ate the M&M's right away did poorly in school and in life; the children who were able to wait longer did better, and the children who waited until the adult returned with more M&M's were exceptionally successful in school and life. They found that the ability to delay gratification was the single most important factor in success, compared to IQ, physical capabilities, race, sex, etc. They also noted the variety of coping mechanisms that the children used to avoid eating the M&M's. Some covered their eyes, stood far away, sang, tapped, yelled, etc.

Discuss how we have succeeded or failed at delaying gratification in our lives. Is the belief in an afterlife the ultimate delayed gratification? Is buying now and paying later part of it? Do the men who have the ability to save and those that don't see a correlation? How much has this ability or lack of it affected our lives? If any men dropped out before the eight weeks, was it because they were unable to work first in order to find a reward later? This criterion can be applied to everything from income to parent-child relationships.

Depression

Almost everyone suffers from some depression now and then. It can be mild or intense. Men are often embarrassed by it because our culture's image of a man says that he is virile, energetic, and active. Depression appears to be the opposite. Whenever I see exaggerated cultural stereotypes, I wonder why society is so determined to project such an image. What is it covering up? In this case, I think it is covering up the fact that we as men do become depressed and we have difficulty controlling it. Be free in your group to talk about it. Discuss personal coping mechanisms that have worked. These can include medications and what their side effects are. You might be surprised at how many men are or have been on medication for depression, yet have never told another man.

And consider this, the extremely depressed are most likely not in your group. This is an issue that we as a society have not recognized or dealt with well.

Drugs

This meeting topic can be about our personal histories with drugs, ranging from coffee and sugar to debilitating drug addiction. Honesty is especially important here, whether there are positive, negative, or no ramifications to your use.

What about the use of drugs in religious or spiritual work? Are traditions like serving wine at a Catholic Mass or Peyote at the American Church of the Peyote Way, or tea at the Buddhist tea ceremony all acceptable practices or not? What role do these drugs play? What is the difference between the roles? Does the use of coffee after services among Lutherans constitute a spiritual community's use of a common drug? Where are the boundaries of acceptable drug use for each of us, and how did we arrive at these conclusions? We may never agree, but exploring these issues is important. Explorations help us understand ourselves and accept differences among the men.

Floor Plans

I practice architecture so, at one of our meetings, I passed out graph paper and asked each man to draw a boyhood home. I told them to scale each box on the paper as a 2 foot by 2 foot square. I then told them the size of the room that we were in, 20 feet by 30 feet. So if their bedroom was about a quarter the size of that room, it would be 10 feet by 15 feet. The drawing of their bedroom would be 5 squares by 7 or 8 squares. It doesn't have to be precise. We were amazed by the memories that this exercise brought back. When we were done, we talked about what we did where. It was like visiting each boy's home.

This can also be varied with every guy drawing his perfect dwelling.

Fathers

The meeting(s) can be about our fathers, our children, or both. What would you change about either relationship? What are the best parts of the relationship? What did you learn from your father? This is difficult for men who never knew their fathers or had fathers that were not there for them.

If members don't have children, the question could be, "If I had children what would I want the relationship to be?" For men who are fathers the question might be, "What do I wish was different about my relationship with my children?" Is the relationship different between fathers and sons and fathers and daughters?

Food

This topic can be about everything from food addictions, losing weight, or the best foods we ever ate. What do we want our relationship with food to be? Look up the original definition of gluttony as written by Pope Gregory as one of the seven deadly sins. Did you know seasoning or the use of a sauce was once considered gluttony? Franciscan monks were once instructed to sprinkle ashes on their food so that they would not be tempted to enjoy it. Does anyone feel guilty about enjoying their food, or not eating everything on their plate? Love-hate and guilt relationships with food can be daily issues. Do we understand why we eat, what we eat?

A more playful take on this is doing a blindfolded taste test. You will find that the range of ability to identify flavors is very diverse, and that some men have the ability to identify one flavor but not another.

God

This is God, not necessarily religion. Who or what is God? Nothing! Everything! A father image! Nature! Is He good? Is He male? Is He evil? Is man a reflection of His goodness or His maliciousness? Feel free to challenge, to dig deep without being offensive. In this kind of discussion reflective conversations are great. For example, "I hear you telling me that … if that is true then why do I also hear you say… To me, it sounds like a contradiction, is it?" The purpose is to help men clarify their thinking into a consistent statement of faith. Men in Buddhist and Christian monasteries have used such questioning for centuries in order to sharpen their understanding.

Hobbies

From woodworking to astrology, are our hobbies our bliss? What are our hobbies and why do we do them (or not if we don't)? What is keeping us from turning them into our profession? This can bring up a lot of issues related to work and pleasure. Some men believe that work must be unpleasant or it isn't real work. If all our hobbies produce a product (like woodworking as opposed to hiking), what does that tell us about ourselves? Hobbies reveal a lot about who we are.

Loss

Loss could be the topic of a hundred meetings: loss of a loved one, loss of innocence, loss of faith, loss of love, loss of a relationship, loss of money, loss of respect, loss of our youth, and many more. Loss in a man's life occurs often, and each time it places a mark on our souls. How do we heal? How has the experience changed us? These can be emotional meetings because often we have not confronted our losses; we have simply dismissed them as inevitable.

Love

What are the differences between romantic love and philanthropic love? What are the differences between, love, lust, and infatuation? For you has love been painful, as some poets say, or blissful as others claim?

Here is a challenge. Dr. A. G. Luker, a behavioral scientist, proclaimed that love did not exist, because it was not measurable. Try to come up with a working definition for love that is objectively measurable and that everyone agrees on. Doing so will help you examine how each man understands love.

Mission Statement

After about a year, it might be time to decide who you are as a group. A way to do this is to write a "Mission Statement." While these have been over used by organizations when they are trying to motivate folks, a mission statement can be a great vehicle for understanding what the group is. This is a huge topic. If you decide to do it, you might work on it over many meetings, devoting only part of each meeting to it. There is a lot of information available to help you. Start with a search for "Mission Statement Generators" or read the reviews of the many books on the topic. Come up with a plan and start your mission.

Money

This topic is the single most sensitive topic in our current society. Men are often measured by how much they make or how much they have. There are a lot of studies about men and money that could be used as a basis for discussion. For example, most men believe that if they made 30% more, they would be happy. This is true no matter how much they make. Also, is saving important? When did the men who have savings start saving? Often our attitudes about money started early. The Bible says in 1 Timothy 6:10: "For the love of money is the root of all evil." Is the "money" or "the love of it" the problem? Do you equate money with power? How do you feel when you give money away? Is winning better with a cash prize? Would you work if you had all the money you wanted? What power does money give, and what is it powerless to do?

Mothers

This is a good meeting near Mother's Day. There is a line in Robert Bly's *Iron John*, where the caged wild man asks the boy to release him. The boy tells The Wildman that he doesn't know where the key is. The Wildman tells the boy it is under his mother's pillow where she hid it years ago, and instructs him to steal it and let him out. This is where the real adventure begins. The group might want to read the chapter before the meeting. Did your mother lock up the Wildman in you? What kind of a man did she want you to be? Did you meet her expectations? Was she there for you when you needed her? How has the relationship changed over time? What haven't you told your mother?

Movies

Talk about great movies and what you got from them, or watch one.

Mythologies

If you're a devotee of Joseph Campbell, I need not say much more. If not, consider reading his *A Hero with a Thousand Faces*, or *Iron John* by Robert Bly. Mythological tales and fairy stories are filled with symbolic language that helps us see and understand our own journey.

Nurturing

What is nurturing? Generally, it is considered a more feminine attribute than a masculine one. Why is this so? How do we as men define it? I like defining it as: "Providing for another what they need even at one's own expense." The typical examples are parents who give up time, sleep, or comfort for the good of a child. A women breast feeds by giving her child nourishment even during circumstances when she is deprived herself. But I'm going to take this one step further. Wouldn't the greatest act of nurturing be to give up one's life so that another can live?

In one survey, men said more often than women that they were willing to die to save their child, another man's child, the mother of a child, and even the father of a young child. Checking their data against actual events like shipwrecks and other disasters, the researchers found the responses correlated with actions taken by each sex. Men gave up their seats on life boats, passed on life preservers, covered children with their bodies in a storm, died saving children in fires, and went without food more often than did women. Is there a difference between heroics and nurturing or are they manifestations of the same attribute expressed differently by men and women? How else do men nurture by giving up aspects of their life?

This topic can also be about how were we nurtured or not nurtured and what effects it had on us.

Poetry

Everyone brings some meaningful poetry to read, or writes a poem based on a photo clipped from a magazine.

Politics

There is so much politics in the world already you may want to avoid it in the group. But if you decide to go for it anyway, remember to use all of the communication guidelines. These topics can get heated and misunderstandings can happen. Remember, everyone wants a better world; the disagreement is how best to get there. Also, remember that so far, no one path has worked all that well, and yet the world is still functioning. So everyone must be wrong on some points and right on others. No yelling, these men are your brothers.

Potluck

This might be a meeting or an event. We have occasionally had events where partners were invited. But you can also simply have everyone bring food to a meeting. Eating together is a primal bonding event. As a variation on this, one night we made an outdoor fire and roasted large chunks of marinated meat on sticks. I'm certain that men a half million years ago would have felt right at home. You should make accommodations for vegetarians.

Procrastination

When you finally get around to talking about procrastination, remember this: one study asserts that one in five people suffer from clinical procrastination. This means to a level that it affects their quality of life, work performance, relationships, etc. (the same criteria that would be applied for clinical depression, alcohol, or drug abuse). While everyone procrastinates sometimes or about some tasks, more people suffer from clinical procrastination than any other diagnosis. It is often connected with other issues. Is it a symptom, or is it a cause? Is it genetic, a disease, or a character flaw? How do we cope with it? How do you cope with others who constantly procrastinate at work or in their private life?

Regret

For most men at the end of their lives they regret not trying more than trying and failing. What do we regret most? How can we avoid future regrets?

Religion

Do you practice a religion? What religion were you reared in? Have you changed? If you don't practice a religion, why not? What do you believe?

Sex

This can have so many topic variations; it could be a book on its own. So, I will just include it as I'm sure everyone will be able to think of at least twenty meetings. This could be a topic for a brainstorming meeting. Remember, when dealing with this topic, confidentiality and understanding are especially important.

Shame

Some men were shamed as boys and have lived under its shadow throughout their lives. It is the force that prevents them from being authentic. Other men have moral compasses that are out of alignment because they lack the ability to feel shame. Shame can have positive effects on our lives, or we can be captured by its dark side. We need to understand this powerful force. What actions are we rightfully ashamed of and what events have we been wrongly shamed by? How are shame and guilt related in your life?

Siblings

If you have had siblings, how do you think they have affected you? Discussions of birth order, how you got along as children, and how it is different now are good topics. For men who are only children, did you like it or did you long for siblings?

Singing

If you do this at a meeting, make sure everyone enjoys singing, will be accepted at any level of ability, or is comfortable not singing along. Some men cannot audibly match pitch or follow rhythm, and for them being asked to sing can be as uncomfortable as asking a guy who has never played basketball to participate in a pick-up game.

Songs

Have every man bring a song that speaks to him or has a particular attachment for him. Another way of doing this meeting is the leader shares the lyrics and music of an artist and time is taken to talk about each song. This works best if the leader provides the lyrics printed out.

Spiritual Path

In most groups, there will be a variety of spiritual paths that the men are pursuing. These paths can be broader than specific religions. For example, a man might be a Lutheran, yet finds meditation to be spiritually enlightening. Design this meeting to discuss the pathways the men are using, what they have investigated, and how they work for them. In addition to meditation, they might include prayer, yoga, tantric practice, study, reading, asceticism, psychotropic substances, vision quests, or some of the many mystical practices such as, Kabbalah, Hasidism, Shingon, Tibetan, Zen, Jhana, Christian mysticism, Gnosticism, Vedanta, Bhakti, Kashmir Shaivism, Sufism, Irfan, or Moksha.

Sporting Events

It doesn't have to be a major league game. We have had great times at our local minor league ballpark. It's the hotdogs, the cheering, and the camaraderie that bonds men together, not the price of the ticket.

Wildman Within

Bly, Campbell and others have written extensively on this topic. Meeting(s) could talk about everything from the wildest things we have done to the wildest things we ever wanted to do. How do we control our Wildman? When do we let him out and when do we restrain him? Do we perceive of our Wildman as dangerous, like the Incredible Hulk, or playful like Pan? Is he our personification of freedom, or is he representative of a primitive beast? Here our feelings should take front and center; by talking about our Wildman we may discover a lot about who we are.

Work (Our Jobs)

In our society, many men believe that they are their profession. We learn in school that there <u>are</u> plumbers, mailmen, doctors, and lawyers. We are not told that there are men who <u>practice</u> plumbing, mail delivery, medicine, or law. No wonder we think we are our profession. By taking off our work costumes and leaving our roles behind for a while, we can find out who we are as men. This can be very difficult for some men. For some, the role has been deeply infused. For example, it can be nearly impossible for some priests, ministers, and rabbis to be just another guy with all the failings, joys, and fears of a man. Think how hard it would be for a governor or a senator. I have observed that if a man believes he has been "called" to his profession, he is more likely to identify himself with that profession than a man who believes he has chosen his profession. Men who have been forced into their work because it was the only job they could get have almost no identification with their profession. A related topic is, what is the difference between a job and a profession?

This could also be addressed using role play. For example one could exaggerate oneself or someone from another profession. Or, one could act as if suddenly unemployed, or barred from practicing one's profession. How would you introduce yourself when someone asked "What are you?" How would you feel?

Another way to approach this topic: If you were to write something other than your profession on a business card that described who you are, what would it be? You could give out small cards and have everyone design the business card of who they really are. If you did this without a name, put the cards in a hat and drew one out, could the men guess who you are by what you wrote?

Xenophile and Xenophobe

Some men are interested in foreign cultures; others are afraid of them. This topic can be interesting when asking, "What cultures (time and place) would you like to have lived in and what ones would you fear to live in?" Maybe we all are a bit xenophilic (attracted to foreign peoples, cultures, or customs) and xenophobic (fearful of foreign peoples, cultures, or customs).

Zenith

I have read that men have less than ten peak experiences in their lives. Winning a Gold Medal at the Olympics might be one, or perhaps when Pablo Picasso finished Guernica and realized that it was a masterpiece might be another. But typically there are others. These are times when we are so into the experience and so certain of the outcome that we feel immortal. What were some peak moments in each man's life and why? How was it readjusting back to mortal life? Can we make these moments happen or are they gifts?

Chapter 14:
Men Exiting – Men Joining

Men will leave the group for many reasons; they die, move, or simply decide they no longer want to be a member. Some exiting is unavoidable, but sometimes it is an indication of failure. Groups fail for various reasons. Two of the most common are failure to embrace conflict and failure to be authentic. These two aspects are the hardest to maintain individually and in the group.

Failure to Embrace Conflict

No ten men are going to agree on everything. Pretending to agree or deciding that expressing a different opinion will result in not being liked or hurting someone's feelings is dishonest. You have the tools to disagree. Disagreeing doesn't mean you have to hold your ground. For example, the group decides to go out for dinner. Bob says great, how about Pizza Joe's? You hate Pizza Joe's, but you say nothing. "Anyone else have any suggestions?" You say nothing. You go and hate it. You resent not having a voice. You decide these guys never do what I want; this isn't the group for me. If you don't want to go, say so. Even if after discussion you all still go, you will feel better about it than not having said anything. Having voiced your feelings, the guys will know that you like them even more than you hate Pizza Joe's and your presence is your gift to them. Or you can decide to pass and not go to Pizza Joe's, and the men must respect your individual choice.

This was purposely a somewhat simple example. Real issues are often more complex. But failure to speak up results in resentment and a failure to bond. Secret grudges that are held manifest themselves in odd and destructive ways. I have almost come to blows with my best friends, men I would die for. But we value the relationship enough to confront each other when we need to without walking away. If your group values and trusts each other to be there when the dust clears, then you have a group. If someone leaves with resentments, there is a failure. The failure might be with the man or the group. Be honest and recommit to express yourself.

Failure to be Authentic

The group is a community where we take off our masks. If we can't put away the roles we play as we "strut and fret our hour upon the stage,"* then we are not in the Men's Hut. Some men find it harder to trust than do others. A breach of confidentiality makes trust even more difficult. If a man's revelations of "who he is" results in ridicule or condemnation, he will build a stronger shell. That shell for some is such thick armor that attempts to remove it are just too painful, and the man decides that it isn't worth the effort. And, perhaps for some men, it is the way it must be. Only they can decide.

* William Shakespeare: Macbeth (Scene V)

The Process of Leaving

If a man announces that he is leaving, he has already thought it over, and typically struggled with it. He may have worked on the issue at an earlier meeting. It is not the role of anyone to try and talk him out of it. Accept it. Men who need to be convinced are not on the same journey that the other men are. At the first meeting, the sixth guideline that every man agreed to was to attend an exit meeting if he decided to leave the group. His presence at his exiting meeting is important to the group. If a man leaves without saying "Goodbye," it leaves a hole in the group that takes longer to heal. Ask the man to come to the next meeting for his exit.

The meeting begins as usual; the leader announces the name of the man who will be leaving the group. The exiting man can talk about his decision, what the group has meant to him, and where it failed. Or he can just say he is leaving. Do not argue with him. He is right for what he perceives. There is no way anyone can have any insight into his feelings and thoughts. Thank him for the information.

Then have a round where every man takes a turn to talk about any unfinished business. Say what you need to, but also try to say what you will miss by his absence. Try to end on a positive note.

Then the man exiting should address each man, also saying what he needs to say and what he will miss about each man.

If you have a meeting closing ritual, do it now and the man leaves. If you plan to maintain contact, assure him that your friendship will not be ending. A functioning men's group does not shun members who leave. If, however, you have little in common with him and you don't plan to maintain contact, do not pretend that you will.

A new meeting starts with the remaining members by repeating the opening ritual.

At this meeting, some or all of the men may want to work on the loss; or take time to do a round about it. The loss of a group member is like any loss. Talk about your feelings. Then move on.

Sometimes when someone leaves, the group becomes inhibited. The men become careful, fearful that they might offend or make someone else so uneasy as to cause them to leave, too. Don't get comfortable, or the group will become meaningless. Keep it challenging or you will lose not only members, you may lose the purpose of the group.

Replacing Lost Members or Adding New Members

If your group started with ten or eleven men there is no need to replace a missing member until the group is down to six or seven, or a year has passed before adding new members. Before you start, understand that this will be a new group of equals. It is important that the new men don't feel like the junior class coming in. Conceive of the process as the group reforming rather than accepting new members.

The actual process is almost the same as when the group first started, except this time work together to decide what the common themes in your group are, and work together to design a post that everyone agrees on. Don't be surprised if this takes some time and causes some frustration. You might need to use your communication, conflict, and compromise skills here.

Divide up the work for posting, but have one man responsible for communications. If it can be someone different from the first time, that is better. As men apply, divide up the face-to-face interviews. If possible, have two men from the group share each interview. The most difficult aspect of the face-to-face is evaluating the man, and if he is not a qualified candidate, letting him know. Remember, he might not be right for your group, but he will be right for his group. So he can start his own. If you think that he has neither the ability nor motivation to do so, then he would not have made a good member of your group either. Remember to get a commitment from each man to attend the first eight meetings.

After the men are selected, restart the group repeating the first eight meetings in this manual. There are no short cuts. For the men who have been through it before, you will learn more. For the new guys, it will put them on an equal footing. Existing members may find what they wrote in their notes when they started interesting, and it will give them greater empathy with the new men.

In eight weeks, it will begin to feel like an authentic community again.

Don't be surprised if some existing men leave the group at this point. For some men, the challenges of reforming can seem daunting and the understanding that the group will be different will weigh heavily on them. For others, they have been thinking about leaving for a while and now will seem appropriate. If the group is down to four or five, it will most likely fall apart anyway. So reforming and bringing it to 10-12 members is your best option to ensure a healthy group even if you lose some guys. Like the first time, this is a new adventure.

Your group might have to repeat this process three or more times over the first ten years before the group stabilizes. Remember, you are forming a community, not just a club. In the end, you will have life-time friends. Remember what they say in India: "In the end, it will all turn out right. If it is not right, well, then it is not the end."

Chapter 15:
Sharing with Other Men's Groups

Website

On the website www.MensGroupManual.com I will be posting additional information that may be helpful. Meeting Topics, Outings, and Rituals are some of the topics I will place under the **Sharing Information** menu. There may be additional selections added over time. If you would like to contribute ideas for the website that you think other groups will be interested in please send them to me.

Facebook

On the website there is a Facebook Group link. I have kept the Facebook group fairly open for anyone to post. Feel free to use it and let's see together how it develops. If changes to the Facebook Group page are needed in the future, the information will be posted on the www. MensGroupManual.com site.

Men's Groups in Your Area

If you wish, I will place your contact information under the **Men's Groups in Your Area** menu. It can be placed there when you are starting a group and/or there permanently. Over the years we have joined with other groups for drumming sessions, hikes, and other events. It's invigorating to exchange ideas and it is always fun to meet new friends.

If there is no group in your area, start one. You can!

I wish you all the best of success and let me know how you are doing.

CPSIA information can be obtained
at www.ICGtesting.com
Printed in the USA
LVOW05s0924050117
519815LV00032B/455/P